MEMOIRS of

"My Army Days During the Cold War

1965 Through 1968"

Second Edition

Patrick Roy

Contents

Introduction 1

Chapter One Graduation Week, June 1965 2

Chapter Two Road Trip To Fort Dix, New Jersey 11

Chapter 3 Arriving at Fort Dix, New Jersey 16

Chapter Four Rifle Range Training 23

Chapter Five World's Fair, New York 29

Chapter Six Graduation Day 32

Chapter Seven Advanced Training Fort Polk, Louisiana 36

Chapter Eight Starting Two Weeks Leave 44

Chapter Nine Hartford 51

Chapter Ten Crossing the Atlantic Ocean 57

Chapter Eleven Arriving in Frankfurt 64

Chapter Twelve My first alert 76

Chapter Thirteen Berchtesgaden 82

Chapter Fourteen Berchtesgaden Continued The Trip to The Salt Mines 89

Chapter Fifteen A regular day 1/36th Infantry 100

Chapter Sixteen Thanksgiving Dinner 106

Chapter Seventeen European Infantry Badge, Testing 110

Chapter Eighteen Visit To The Dispensary 119

Chapter Nineteen Preparing For a Two-Week Field Maneuvers 128

Chapter Twenty Grafenwöhr Two Weeks Field Maneuvers 135

Chapter Twenty-One Getting Together with My Twin 151

Chapter Twenty-Two Alert War Games 157

Chapter Twenty-Three England 166

Chapter Twenty-Four Holiday To the Coast 177

Chapter Twenty-Five The Academy 183

Chapter Twenty-Six The Academy 189

Chapter Twenty-Seven Koplin Guard 194

Chapter Twenty-Eight Weekend In Amsterdam 198

Chapter Twenty-Nine NATO Exercise 208

Chapter-Thirty Radio School 217

Chapter Thirty-One Transfer to Brigade 232

Chapter Thirty-Two Emergency leave 237

Chapter Thirty-Three Transfer to Division Headquarters 246

Chapter Thirty-Four Field Training 252

Chapter Thirty-Five ETS Back to The States 266

About The Author 273

About Me 274

MEMOIRS OF

"My Army Days During The Cold War"

1965 Through 1968

By

Patrick Roy

Introduction

I am a Waterville, Maine native. I am 77 and have wanted to write a book for several years. It took me three years to write this book. The book is about my life in the United States Army stationed in West Germany during the Cold War. Many soldiers have served in West Germany during the Cold War. If you were stationed there during the Cold War, if you purchased the book, it will bring back memories. I graduated from High School in 1965. I did not get along with my mother and had to leave home. Enlisting in the Army allowed me to travel throughout Europe, and the government paid for it. I got to travel to many places. I would never have been able to go to places on my own. I learned a lot and grew up at a fast pace. I've hiked up the Alpes, traveled to England, sat down with the Mayor of Bury, England, and presented with the Key to the City. You will read about the times I cheated death twice and broke the chain of command a couple of times.

I am sure you will enjoy reading this book.

www.PatrickJamesRoy.com

Chapter One

Graduation Week, June 1965

The time was getting close to my graduation day, class of 1965. I attended the local high school in my hometown, Waterville, Maine, for four years. It was four long years, and like most 18-year-olds, I could not wait to live independently.

I could not wait to leave home and start a new adventure in this vast, wide world. In addition to attending high school, I worked at the Waterville Morning Sentinel, about half a mile from where I lived. I have worked for the morning newspaper in the circulation department mailroom since I was sixteen. I worked forty hours a week as a full-time employee, earning $1.35 per hour. My hours at the newspaper were 10:00 p.m. till 6:00 a.m., after working eight hours at the newspaper before going home. I would deliver newspapers because I also had a paper route with fifty-two customers.

After graduating from high school, I intended to move to Hartford, Connecticut, hoping to find a job at Pratt & Whitney, which makes airplane parts. While attending high school, I took shop courses intending to work for a production manufacturing plant. Uncle John lived in Hartford, Connecticut, with his family. His wife, Aunt June, and their four children had agreed I could live with them until I was employed. Once I had put enough money away, I would live independently. My mother had a different plan for my future. Mom was ruffling my feathers; like most boys leaving high school, I sought more out of life than living in a small town like Waterville. Waterville had a population of a little over 16,000 residents (about the seating capacity of Madison Square Garden).

My mother and I disagreed when it came to my future. We were constantly arguing about any little thing that came up. I wanted to do something with my life besides living in the same house under my parents' roof. I would do anything to find a way to leave home, which was my determination. We could no longer live under the same roof. Mom was a controller, seeing how she controlled my dad for many years. Dad was a great family provider and a noticeably quiet person. As you might guess, my mother ran the household. Graduation was just a few days away. Preparing for the Senior Prom was vital to me at the time. Now, I would have to find a way to move out of the house and pursue my own life.

I went to Levine's men's clothing store on Main Street in town. My uncle Roland, my mother's youngest brother, worked as a sales clerk at Levine's. He always treated me very well; I went to the store to order a Tux for the prom. Uncle Roland was a significant help, as he knew all my measurements. Being continually active, I was not a considerably large person at 18 years old. I only weighed 123 pounds and had a 26-inch waist.

Prom night was upon us. Fred (a friend throughout high school) played in a local 4-piece band with three other boys from school. Fred and I double-dated for the prom; we dated sisters Martha, and Jan. Jan was my date for prom night; Jan and I went out together for several months. My mother was against me dating anyone. I went to Levine's early that afternoon to pick up my rented Tux. Uncle Roland gave me a special family deal of only ten dollars for the rented Tux.

Fred and I were good friends, and I hung around with him and the band he played with, The Chevelles. Every time the band had a gig, my dad would allow me to use the family car to move the band's equipment. The guys would fill the tank with gas whenever they asked to use the vehicle. Being the only person in the group with a driver's license made me the official driver. Gas was about thirty-five cents per gallon in those days.

After taking the rented tux home, I headed to the local Army recruiters' office next door to the Morning Sentinel, where I worked in the circulation department. I wanted to leave home so desperately that I was willing to give up four years of my life to serve my country. After a long talk with the recruiter, Sergeant Kirk knew I wanted to join the Army and start a new life away from home. He explained some of the benefits I would receive when enlisted. After a few hours of talking and watching videos, we got to business. Sergeant Kirk asked me which country I wanted to go to after training. I hoped to be given England as my first choice. Sergeant Kirk told me if I wanted England or Germany, I'd have to sign up for four years. I had made a pen pal friend from Bury, England, a town in central England. My second choice was Germany. I started writing to Gail after I heard her name and address on a Boston Radio Station, WLBZ, in 1964; she was looking for a pen pal from the States.

Sergeant Kirk showed me a few videos about Army life. I would see the world, which was the chance of a lifetime. I was convinced to enlist in the United States Army. I was unaware of what was happening in Vietnam, except that we were at war. Currently, entering the military is extremely easy. Enlisting for four years would allow me to choose where the Army would send me. Had it not been for enrolling, the possibility of getting drafted would have been great.

After leaving the recruiter's office that evening, I wrote Gail a letter to tell her about my enlistment in the United States Army. And would arrive in Germany in about six months. I plan to visit Gail in

Bury, England, to meet her and her family after I arrive in Germany. Therefore, I hoped to transfer to England, but Germany would work out just fine.

After spending time with Sergeant Kirk, I left to prepare for the prom. Before the senior prom, Fred and I would take our dates out for dinner. I had made a reservation for the four of us at Baldacci Restaurant in Skowhegan. The restaurant was two towns away, about eighteen miles from home.

I headed home to get ready for the prom. I was excited. (Did I forget to mention I have a twin brother, Gil?). Mom was excited for both of us boys to graduate from high school. Even though we had completed high school, Mom did not want us to leave home. But that was not going to stop me from leaving. I would not let my family know I had joined the Army until after graduation. My oldest brother was already in the military and was currently in Virginia. Knowing this would upset my mother. I would not mention my subsequent Army enlistment to my mother so she would not get upset before graduation.

Graduation was upon us; it was five o'clock, and we had a restaurant reservation for 6:00 p.m. at Baldacci. As always, Dad allowed me to use the family car, a 1961 Chevy. I picked Fred up at his home within minutes. Then, I drove to pick up the girls in Fairfield. Martha and Jan looked terrific. We went to the restaurant and arrived at the right time for our reservation. It took us about one hour for dinner, which was great. After dinner, we headed to Waterville High School for the prom.

We were not the first to arrive at Waterville High School at about 8:00 p.m. Our school mascot was the "Purple Panthers," and all hall decorations were purple and white. A live band was playing, they were great. You might say I was surprisingly good at dancing in those days back in the sixties. Dances were a weekly thing for me. At the time, I would go to two dances a week.

We had a wonderful time at the dance. I saw Gil (my twin) and his date having an exciting time; it looked like everybody was having a wonderful time at the prom dance. We danced a lot, and we had a wonderful time. I danced with other girls, and Jan did the same with the other boys. There was a small refreshment table at the back of the dance hall, which served some soft drinks and light snacks. We left the prom after two and a half hours.

After the dance, I drove to a place to park at the Devil's Chair on Quarry Road in Waterville behind the Thayer Hospital. It did not take long for the car windows to fog up. Jan and I were hot and sweaty in the front seat. We got into kissing and fondling of each other. I told Jan we should not keep a long-distance relationship, as we would be apart for at least four years. After being out on a dirt road making out for about an hour, I drove the girl's home and then drove Fred to his home. I arrived home at about 1:00 a.m. and went to bed. It felt good not having to go to work because I had just quit my job.

Being 18 years old, I was looking forward to leaving home and starting a new chapter in my life. My family is a committed Catholic, and Churchgoers never miss attending Sunday church services. I never missed a Sunday morning going to Church until one day, my oldest brother Don taught me how to get out of going to the Church. One day before attending Church service a couple of years back, Don asked if I wanted to skip Church and go to Foxes' Pool Hall on Silver Street, near the Church. Missing the Church service put guilt on me, but being sixteen, I would be alone in a few years and would be leaving home anyway. My mother would ask what the priest's sermon was, and we would go to the Church on our way home after leaving the pool hall. I'd go inside the Church building to get the Sunday Church newsletter. The newsletter always outlined the Sunday sermon.

Graduation day is finally here. Gil (my twin brother) and I were finally going to graduate. It was four long years in high school. I was not an "A" student, but I was good enough to pass all my grades. My brother Gil and I did not have anything in common except being twin brothers. He had his group of friends, and I had my group of friends.

Mom and Dad drove us to the high school for the great moment we had been waiting for. All students who were to be graduates were to meet in the gym for the line-up, and then we headed to the auditorium to our seats.

Once in the gym, the organizers prepared us to march into the general auditorium, where hundreds of family members were present.

We had 305 students graduating that evening—the largest class ever to leave Waterville High School, a record that still stands today.

After the graduation ceremony, Gil and I went home with the family. Both Gil and I were thrilled we had finished high school. Mom had a graduation gift for both of us: a Timex Watch. My brother did not have a long-term plan like mine. Waiting to leave home and go out into the unknown world was what I wanted at this time. I wanted to travel and see the world. I was Dad's favorite; I would collaborate with Dad on Saturdays. He did off-the-books work putting T.V. antennas.

The next evening, I went out with friends. I was using Dad's car as always. We headed to an out-of-town auditorium about an hour's drive to another dance location. This location would be the last time I ever went to this auditorium in Brewer for a dance. We had fun at the dance; usually, meeting girls was not hard to do. After the dance, we packed the car and left for home on the one-hour drive. We arrived home at about midnight. On Saturday night, both parents were home watching a late show on TV and being alone with my parents once again. I asked Mom if it would be okay to move to Hartford to see what she would say. She had not changed her mind. Then I told her I was leaving in two days and would be gone for a while. Of course, this led to an argument. She was telling me I was too young to be on my own. My dad was quiet; he wanted to see me do something for myself.

That's right; I will be leaving town on a bus heading to Fort Dix, New Jersey, for basic training, as I have joined the Army. Mom had no words to say and ran to her bedroom, upset. After going to bed, I could hear Mom and Dad talk about what might have made me join the Army.

Early the following day, I woke up, showered, had a good breakfast, and left for the day. I wanted to say goodbye to my closest friends when evening came, and I visited a female friend. Her name was Donna, and she lived in the next town in Fairfield. Donna was going to be a senior in high school. I only knew Donna for a couple of years; she liked me, or should I say she had a crush on me. My evening with Donna was terrific; we did some make-out stuff. She let me feel her up as she did the same to me. Feeling her up made me extremely excited. I always remember Donna because she was the first girl who let me feel her naked breasts. Donna was a great kisser, and she also knew this would be the last time we would see each other. Donna not only let me touch her naked breasts but also pulled my face to her chest to allow me to kiss and suck on her breasts. Donna's allowing me to touch her was the highlight of my life, and this is one day I will never forget it.

It was the last time I saw Donna. I then headed home for the night to pack. Mom and Dad waited for me to spend the last few hours with them when I arrived home. We talked for a couple of hours, and it was getting late. I had to get some rest and sleep as the bus was leaving at 10:00 a.m. I said good night to my parents and then went to my room. I pack just the personal-care products I was allowed. I have been told not to pack too much and no clothing, as I would get all-new uniforms, shoes, and boots.

Chapter Two

Road Trip To Fort Dix, New Jersey

I hardly slept a wink that night. I got out of bed at around 7:30 a.m., went to the bathroom, showered, and dressed for the day. Today would be different and exciting, as I would be alone for the first time. I would have no family to turn to if I needed personal help.

As I descended the stairs for breakfast, I could smell the aroma of bacon cooking as Mom prepared my last breakfast there for a long while.

Dad drove us off in the family car toward the Greyhound bus station less than half a mile from our home. Mom and Dad were the only ones to see me off at the bus station; driving to the station took less than five minutes. Dad parked the car right in front of the Greyhound bus station. It was warm outside. And once inside the building, there was no difference in the temperature. It was warm inside the station, and air conditioning was not the norm back in the sixties. In the '60s, air conditioning was not in every car or home.

Entering the bus depot, I advanced toward the check-in desk to see what time the bus going to Portland was leaving. The ticket man told me the bus would be on time and leave at 10:00 am sharp. The first leg of my trip was to stop in Portland at the induction center's office. The induction center would be where I would get sworn into the United States Army. The Greyhound bus should be on time with two stops on the way; the first was in Augusta, and the second was in Lewiston, then onto Portland.

Looking out the window, I saw the bus arriving at the station. The destination marker on the bus was to Portland. Like most 18-year-olds, I was getting extremely excited. Dad handed me a twenty-dollar bill he could not afford. Then Mom and Dad hugged me warmly and told me to be careful and to call anytime and often. Mom was crying, and even at this time, she asked me not to go. I told her it was too late—living at home would not work for me. I headed outside toward the bus. After entering the bus, I sat about halfway on it. Sergeant Kirk advised me not to sit at the rear of the bus as the toilet was in the back, and sometimes the smell was unpleasant. Looking out the window as the bus was leaving, I saw my mother crying as she and Dad waved goodbye to me.

Not many people were on the bus; some were going to Portland and Boston. The bus arrived at the Augusta depot on Main Street, less than one-half hour from home. About eight people got on board; one was a lovely lady sitting beside me. A name I do not remember; she might have been about 30 years old. We talked about her life. Boy, did she have a messed-up life? She came to Maine as a surprise to visit her long-distant boyfriend. He lived in Maine and worked at a cotton mill at the Bates Manufacturing plant in Augusta. She told me he was not alone when she arrived at her boyfriend's apartment. It looked like another girl was living there with him as she noticed many women's clothing in the apartment, which was clean.

The stop in Augusta was only 10 minutes to unload and reload with new riders. The bus left the station and headed toward Interstate 95 South toward Lewiston. About 45 minutes away. My new friend was very annoying; she talked and talked. I could not change seats as she was sitting in the aisle seat. I closed my eyes and pretended to fall asleep, which did the trick. After pretending to fall asleep, she got up and went to another seat to sit with another male. Thinking she was on the rebound and looking for someone to comfort her was not my thing. It took about 45 minutes to get from Augusta to Lewiston; the stop lasted only a few minutes. The drive to Portland was about one hour from Lewiston.

I met an Army sergeant when the bus arrived at the Portland bus depot. I was not the only person on the bus going to the same place, the Army induction center. Two other boys, or men, were to get sworn into the Army as I was to be.

We were driven to the induction center to get sworn into the United States Army. Once at the center, we were each interviewed separately by different military personnel. It took a couple of hours, and the time went by quickly after being interviewed. I felt immensely proud of myself for becoming an Army soldier; defending this country is honorable for any American citizen. After the interviews and swearing-in, I was given meal tickets to a nearby local restaurant. After eating, I went to a short-term men's boarding home a few blocks from Main Street. I walked from the restaurant to the boarding home, where I stayed for the night.

I did not know Portland had men's boarding homes. The boarding home was off the main street in the downtown area. I had to share a room with one other person that evening. There was some activity I could do while at the boarding home. There was a one-lane bowling alley in the basement of the building. I went down and played a couple of strings. Whoever played this game had to set up the pins manually. So, having two players was a tremendous help in taking turns setting up the pins. I had a morning bus to catch to Fort Dix at 8:00 a.m., so I went to bed at about 11:00 p.m.

I had a 6:00 a.m. wake-up call; I rushed out of bed and cleaned up before leaving the boarding home. After checking out, I headed to the same restaurant I had visited the day before, where I had dinner. After breakfast, I walked to the bus station, about a mile away. I hoped to be the first in line at the bus station to get a good seat near a window. It was about a seven-hour ride and four hundred miles to Fort Dix, New Jersey. No one sat beside me, which was terrific. I had a lot on my mind. What did I do? In just a few months, I would be living in Germany for at least 36 months (three years) on a tour of duty. Oh well, I am out for a new life. I was leaving behind all my family and school friends, especially the band group in the small town of Waterville, Maine. The bus ride went without a flaw, with about three stops on the way. I arrived at the bus station at Fort Dix on time. All I had was a small overnight bag holding my personal belongings.

Arriving at Fort Dix, the bus had stopped. When the bus driver opened the bus doors, a drill instructor jumped onto the bus. He started yelling at all of us as if we had no right as a civilian but the property of the United States Army—he was correct. I became a member of the United States Army.

Chapter 3

Arriving at Fort Dix, New Jersey

As I got off the bus at Fort Dix, I looked like a lost boy who did not know what to expect next—and I was right. I heard some drill instructors yelling at us to move here and then move there. Double time is all we would hear to for the next eight weeks. The DI instructed us to move from the bus and form two columns. We marched to an assembly area where we would be assigned leaders. We stood around and waited for our next move, noticing other buses arriving in the same place. As other recruits got off the buses, they joined our ranks in the formation. About two hundred recruits might have been in this group's formation.

We separated into four groups, which were about fifty soldiers per group. We marched around the base for a while, as they had nowhere to put us for the time being. I heard much talk about how many of us, after training, would be sent orders to war.

The United States engaged in the Vietnam War, and many soldiers occupied the base for training as military troops were in much demand. There were just no vacant barracks for us. It seemed as if they were waiting for a group to graduate from basic training to leave. So our group could move into the barracks.

Many troops missed a meal that afternoon; I had arrived around noon, missing lunch as well. At around 1700 hours, we marched to the consolidated mess hall. It was a huge dining hall that may have held close to two hundred soldiers. We learned to hurry up and wait on this first day in the Army.

After eating dinner, we marched to an open field with scattered trees that offered shade from the sun. Drill instructors told us we should find a place in the shade to sit and rest till they had somewhere for us to go. I spent my first night in the Army sleeping under in the open sky. I was glad it was summertime and did not rain that night. They did make sure we had food for snacks and drinks. There were portable toilets in the area for us to use when needed.

I slept under the stars for my first night in the Army. Waking up with the sun glaring on my face was far from what I had envisioned when I signed up. Sergeant Kirk assured me of three hot meals and a cot, but on the first night in the Army, I had neither. The first night in the Army, I had no bed, not even a sleeping bag. It is not a particularly good first impression. Oh well, this was just the beginning. I soon discovered I would miss other meals and nights in a foxhole instead of a cot. At about 0600 hours, the instructor told us what would happen that morning, but first things first. The instructor got us into what looked like a formation to march us to the mess hall for breakfast. When we arrived at the mess hall, we broke up the company formation and marched in a single file into the mess hall.

Once in the chow line, it might have taken us about 15 minutes to get into the mess hall for breakfast. Upon entering the mess hall, we were to eat our breakfast and get out in fifteen minutes. I was always a fast eater. I had no problem with that timeline. A couple of guys at the table I sat with for breakfast did not finish within those fifteen minutes. The soldiers had to move on as other troops would be seated at the same table we were at.

Once we arrived back outside, we marched to the same grounds we had spent the night before. I met a couple of other enlistees with whom I would spend the next eight weeks (about two months) or so. Many of the troops in this group were smokers, and I had not picked up the habit of smoking. We were to return to a formation once everybody had taken a short break and was outside.

Again, I was in some formation, and the drill sergeant began discussing what we would do as soldiers and who would be with us for the rest of the day. We were first to go to our barracks, home for the next two months; we marched in columns of fours.

We must have walked about two miles when we stopped in front of four buildings. We divided into four groups. Each group was to be assigned a barrack as home. This area would be our company area. Each building had a letter on it, and that would be our home. I was in the third column, my home for the next eight weeks, to the building with the big C on it, or we should call it Charlie Company.

As we entered the building, we were assigned a bunk. We were to stand by the bunk until all personnel were in the barracks. Once, we were all in the barracks, and a different drill instructor, our platoon leader, we were to call him Sergeant. There were 44 bunks in the room, 22 bunks on each side, and a bottom bunk and an upper bunk.

Our barracks, D. I. (Drill Instructor), entered the room. We were to call him Sergeant every time we addressed him. His name was Sergeant Perez; Sergeant Perez stepped to the center of the room and started yelling at us. Nothing I wanted to hear or expected, nor was I told I would be informed this way. He jumped right off and called us a bunch of pussies. When he finished the eight weeks of training with us, we would be soldiers of the United States Army.

I came from a Christian family in a small, quiet town in central Maine. I was not used to being talked down as if I were nothing. Sergeant Perez told us why we were here: to become killing machines. I have never even held a gun in my life. He went on and on for about one hour. After Sergeant Perez finished his introduction speech, we were ordered outside in a platoon formation. Sergeant Perez showed us how to form the platoon formation. He wanted to see four rows of eleven people the size of our platoon. Once in company formation, Sergeant Perez told us we would jog to the supply room about a mile away. Off we started, we double-timed toward the supply room to get some bedding.

Once we returned to our barracks, the DI showed us how to make our bed the way it would have to be every morning. Sergeant Perez should be able to toss a quarter on the bed, and the quarter would have to bounce on the bed. If not, he would flip our mattress onto the floor, and then we'd have to remake the bed to his satisfaction.

After our bed-making lesson, it was time for lunch, and we all headed to the mess hall. To earn our meal, we had to go down the horizontal ladder. Which had about fifteen rungs; this would cause blisters on our hands.

After lunch, we marched *to the supply ho*use for our GI (government-issued) Army clothes. After getting our clothing, we double-timed to the barracks with an Army duffel bag over our shoulder. The group was instructed in a peculiar way to display all our clothing and personal care products for our drill instructor to inspect to make sure we had everything we needed. There would be no room for any personal belongings.

Morning formation was at 0600 hours. I had just gotten to bed, and the morning was upon us. Sharply at 0500 hours, the CQ (Charge of Quarters) came into the room blowing a damn whistle. His announcement was all feet on the floor while yelling, first call. We had one hour to get out for reveille and to go into company formation. Forty-four troopers must hit the bathroom attending to business shit, shower, and shave. We had to shave every morning, even if we did not need to. Before we were to hit company formation, we also had to get our beds made and footlockers in order. I had a complete foot and wall locker with details to follow. We had little time, one hour from the wake-up call at 0500 hours. Once we were out of the barracks, we were not allowed into them until we returned from our 3-mile run.

After breakfast, we assembled into a formation. Our D.I. informed us we were going to the infirmary for medical shots. We entered a classroom and sat in a chair at a desk. Our medical records were presented to us by the administrator. We were to answer all the questions that were in the packet to the best of our knowledge,

After being in the classroom for one hour, we marched out of the class for our shots. Sergeant Perez told us to strip off our shirts and get in line with our shirts in one hand and the medical records in the other. Lining up in a single file, we headed into the building for our shots. I am not sure how many vaccines I received that morning. The doctors and medics used air guns to inject us with the drugs. One physician grabbed my arm, warning me not to move while getting the shots—but it was too late. The air gun slashed me, and blood oozed from the injection site. A quick fix was a band-aid, and I moved on.

After completing the episode at the dispensary, we marched back to the barracks but were not yet allowed back in. Sergeant Perez had us sit on the ground and instructed us on what to expect for the rest of the week.

Sergeant Perez also selected four people to become squad leaders. I was in the third squad; Private Stone was my squad leader. After waiting a little while, we were all to go to the mess hall for lunch. We had to earn that meal before we entered the mess hall. There were horizontal bars we had to go through every time before we entered the mess hall. We must have had fifteen rungs to do, and if we fell off the bars, we'd have to start over again. It was not long before calluses formed on my hands. After lunch, we would go to the arms room to be assigned a weapon, a rifle.

Sergeant Perez taught us how to march in cadence. We were heading to the arms room to be assigned a rifle. Once we arrived, we had to wait for the group ahead of us to go through. While waiting, we were allowed to "light them up if you got them," which would be a daily sound as we were allowed a 10-minute break every hour. Most daily activities would be the same for the next three-plus weeks. Classroom work for the next few weeks felt like being back in school.

We were being trained to become killing machines—"Kill, Kill, Kill." I was eighteen years old and had been going to church every Sunday. For 18 years, my parents taught me to love my neighbor, and now I am being introduced to killing. With my new training, I had to turn against what I thought from my religious beliefs all my life.

Chapter Four

Rifle Range Training

After weeks of classroom training, we went to the rifle range to put theory into practice. After eating a fifteen-minute breakfast, the company was called into formation to receive our daily orders. The day's order informed us that we would be leaving the company area. We were going to the rifle range, and I felt excited about going to the rifle range as I had never fired a gun or a weapon. We are never to call our rifles a gun. It was a rifle or a weapon; this was another first for me.

After being dismissed from the company formation, we headed to the arms room to retrieve our weapons and assemble back in our platoon. Sergeant Perez, our platoon leader, double-timed us to the parade field. Then, we would be boarding troop carriers to move us to the rifle range. The troop carriers resembled cattle trucks equipped with basic seating.

The rifle range seemed like a long-distance drive away. There were small windows in the troop carrier, and we could not see where we were going very well. There were about 30 troops in each troop carrier. Once at the range, we disembarked from the troop carrier. Again, we were to get into company formation with Sergeant Perez's command of "company formation." It did not take long to get into the company and platoon formation. We stood in the same squad line, which was the second squad for me.

We spent most of the day at the range learning about the M14 rifle; there were tables at this range. At these tables, we learned to disassemble and reassemble our M14 rifles. We practiced this until we could reassemble our M14 within a minute. Once the class on the M14 was over, we were going to have some lunch. The mess truck had arrived. The cooks and kitchen police (KP) had everything set up for our meal. We ate well when our meals were available, even when we were out at the ranges.

While getting ready for lunch, we took our combat gear off. Then we set our gear on the ground and tripod our rifles. We were not allowed to leave the area without someone to watch and guard all our equipment. Having learned the hard way before, I avoided being left to watch and guard the gear. I had many times before taken up smoking. As mentioned before, we had a ten-minute break every hour. At break time, the Sergeant or person in charge would say, "Light them up if you got them." If you did not smoke, you'd be the one to watch guard on all the equipment while the others went to class.

That was when I started smoking, and I had never smoked until now—another bad habit inherited from the Army. In the mid-'60s, cigarettes only cost ten cents per pack from the Post Exchange (PX).

After lunch, we were back on the firing lines to use our M14s. We were a team of two with the M14, one trooper with the rifle and the other as the coach. Some of this was taught to us in classrooms a week before coming to the range. I would receive a day pass if we became experienced shooters on our qualifying test. That encouraged me to aim to become an expert in the testing range. The price of getting a day pass would mean I would have the time to go to the World's Fair. I had no earlier experience with a rifle. Wanting so much to qualify as an expert shooter would prepare me for a pass.

Before enlisting in the Army, besides attending high school. I worked full-time for the local newspaper and in a Waterville newspaper's circulation department. A co-worker named Pete and I planned to participate in the 1964 and 1965 World's Fair after graduating high school. Well, that did not pan out. A few weeks before we graduated, Pete and I got into a conflict and called off the trip. If I could make an expert on the range, I would be going to the World's Fair.

After a day of rifle training, we moved back to the barracks on the cattle trucks. I was excited to return to the barracks after a hard day's activity. After putting our weapons away and cleaning up, we would have the last call of the day. After the previous daily company formation, the company commander released us for the day. It was time for the day's last meal.

After dinner, I went back to the barracks. Our squad leader, Private Stone, would have the mail call. Having a subscription to the Waterville newspaper, I knew I would receive mail during mail calls. Once a week, I would receive a letter from my mother, but I did not answer them all.

This one week, I received letters from two girls from home. One of the letters I received was from Bonnie. I had a crush on her back home. Bonnie's letter was welcoming. The other letter I received was from another friend, Ellen, whose dad was a United States senator. Later, her dad was on the voting ballot, running for vice president of the United States.

For the next few weeks, I learned my rifle would be my best friend. There were times we had to attend some classes on other subjects. One of the classes we had to participate in was about how smoking was bad for us. We watched videos about how smoking was not good for our hearts and lungs. Smoking can cause cancer and heart disease. The funny thing was when we went outside for a ten-minute break. The D.I. would announce, "Light them up if you got them." As good as that class was, we needed to attend the course. Another lesson was about Venereal Disease (VD) and the dos and don'ts to protect us from this disease.

Every Friday, we had to clean the barracks for Saturday morning inspection. We had to strip our beds for a linen change. We took everything off the floor and placed the items on the bunks. We wanted to make sure the floors were immaculate for the Saturday inspection. We started our cleaning on Friday evenings. The company platoon that would pass the assessment as the best would be allowed a day pass to go off post. When our platoon wins the evaluation, I will use the day pass. For the whole time, I was in Basic training. I used a day pass twice and two-weekend passes, and there was always something to do on the post. On this occasion, we came in as the second-best in the inspection.

On most Saturday nights, I would spend time at the service clubs. There would be a dance where young ladies from the town would come on post to the dances—being cautious about confident girls because some were interested in having more fun, if you understand what I mean.

One Saturday, I visited my brother Jeff on a weekend pass. He was in Washington, D.C. Buses left the base to go to Washington, DC, at a fair price to the soldiers. The trip to DC was about a seven-hour ride. When arriving at my brother's command, my brother was waiting for me. Jeff took me to his barracks, and he had a bed available as one of his roommates was on leave.

Jeff took me to the building where he worked at the Pentagon, which was a great structure to see. Jeff showed me where he worked. There are seventeen miles of hallways in the Pentagon. The time with my brother was enjoyable and went by like a flash. This weekend was a fast trip, and I enjoyed being with my brother. We did not have too much time to do anything, but he did give me advice about the Army. Some of the things he told me were extremely helpful, and I looked forward to following up with his advice. The following day, we went to the mess hall for breakfast, then back to the bus station and the long ride back to base. I arrived back at Fort Dix late that evening.

Besides testing on the rifle range, we also had tests in the classroom. Classroom exams were a breeze. We have been preparing for the big test for the past few weeks. While visiting my brother, he told me how I could pass the course as an expert shooter. On the range, when a pop-up silhouette appeared, I had to aim at the base of the target. I should hit the dirt just before the silhouette, and it would cause the soil to fly against the target. I tried it, and you guessed it, I made an expert shooter that day and got an overnight pass that would allow me to visit the World's Fair.

Things at the company were slowing down as we were all qualified at some level and became shooters. I was looking forward to the overnight pass to go to the World's Fair as this was a dream of mine; this was a once-in-a-lifetime opportunity. I went to the orderly room to apply for the pass I had earned, an overnight pass I deserved. No problem, except I did not have enough money for a day away from the base. After talking to a few of my roommates about the situation, some offered me cash to enjoy my trip to the World's Fair. The team collected twenty dollars for me; that would be enough with the little bit I had with me.

Chapter Five

World's Fair, New York

I arrived at the Port Authority in New York City around mid-morning. I was only eighteen and had never been to New York City. I had no idea where to go next. I had never heard anything good about New York City. New York City is not the city where I would want to live. I quickly got information from a police officer nearby. I asked him where I could purchase a World's Fair ticket. The police officer directed me to the ticket office.

I arrived at the ticket window to purchase a ticket to the World's Fair grounds and checked to see when the subway would arrive. The subway ride would be the first time in my life that I would be riding on one, but not the last. The Subway was going to be leaving in a few minutes. I would not miss this ride as I wanted to make the best of this day ever. A few minutes before heading down to the underground, I got something to eat. I bought myself a breakfast sandwich and a soft drink. I regretted that I did not have a camera to take some pictures of the city during my visit to the World's Fair. I have no proof of ever attending the fair, only my memories.

After eating a light lunch, I walked over to the platform. I waited for the tram to arrive. Being only 18 years old, I was concerned about my safety. All went fine, but I will tell you, I did not close my eyes for even one minute. I would not suggest that anyone travel alone to New

York City. The subway took me to the fairgrounds. I followed the other people ahead of me to the main gate.

Walking up to the front gate to the Worlds Fairground, there was a two-dollar admitting fee. I spent about 8 hours at the Fair, visiting as many exhibitions as possible. Having a wonderful time at the World's Fair is a day I will never forget. If not for my joining the Army, I would have lost this once-in-a-lifetime opportunity to visit something like a World's Fair. I saw about five exhibitions on this day. Visiting the World's Fair was a big plus. My day at the fair was over, and I had to return to base.

When I arrived at the Port Authority, I checked the schedule for the bus departing to Fort Dix. I had to wait less than an hour for the next bus back to Fort Dix. I grabbed a sandwich and found a place to sit to enjoy my sandwich. Not long after I sat on a bench, some man approached me and asked if he could sit beside me. I told him I did not mind. After I had finished my lunch, the stranger began talking to me. The man asked me where I lived, and I told him where I lived. He asked where I was going and when my bus left Port Authority. I made up a story and told him I was waiting for my older brother, who was coming to meet me as he lived in the area. This guy asked if I wanted to go to his home; he lived in the city. He told me he would pick up a couple of adult movies, and we could watch the shows and have a few drinks. I was aware of people like this person from some of the classes I attended in Basic Training.

I looked at him and said sorry; I have got to call my brother now to remind him I am waiting for him and to come to the Port Authority. I had an idea this jerk wanted more than what he was offering. I got up and went to the other side of the hall. He followed me and pleaded with me to go with him. I told him I was not interested, and he persisted after me. This guy told me he knew I was in the military because my shoes were G.I.-issued. I told him if he did not stop following me, I would call the police on him. There were plenty of police officers and security personnel in the area. That scared him off because he left. I did not see him anymore after that incident.

When arriving at the platform, I saw the bus coming down the roadway. The bus had Fort Dix on its destination marquee. I got on the bus and sat near a window. Arriving on schedule at Fort Dix, I flagged down a taxi and returned to the barracks.

Chapter Six
Graduation Day

Finally, the day of basic training graduation was fast upon us. We had a GI party in the barracks the night before our graduation. We stayed up most of the night cleaning the barracks and preparing for the morning inspection before moving out after graduation.

Many soldiers had already received their orders for their next destination assignment. Some of the soldiers would be moving on for advanced training. Some of us soldiers without travel orders expected to receive them within a week. Meanwhile, we would have moved out of these barracks and sent to a holding center with other troops awaiting their travel orders.

Our D.I. came to inform us what would happen and what he expected of us. After a short speech, the D.I. gave us one hour to prepare and dress for the occasion. Time passed, and we were called into a company formation before marching to the parade field to perform our graduation ceremony in front of the grandstand. The march was about 15 minutes from the parade field. As we marched away, we looked like a group of very sharp soldiers, ready to move out to our graduation location. Many people were in the stands, and knowing my family was there to support me, I am sure they were immensely proud to see their son as a United States soldier. On this occasion, my family came down to see me from the State of Maine, about a 500-mile trip.

As we arrived right in front of the grandstand, we received a standing ovation from the families and guests in the grandstand. I was getting excited to be graduating from Basic Training. I missed my family during my few weeks in the Army and away from home. The graduation commencement started, and there were speakers from our company leaders. After the graduation ceremony, we were dismissed and allowed to visit the families of those attending.

Mom was the first of my family members to get a hold of me. Mom hugged me and kissed me on the cheek. Mom took many pictures of me. She, my dad, and my siblings were immensely proud of me. I already mentioned that I have an older brother stationed in Virginia. My brother Jeff was stationed in Korea and had just returned to the States a few months before I joined the Army. Two of us boys were in the Army simultaneously, which upset Mom because she had two sons in the Army during the Vietnam War, the Korean conflict, and the ongoing Cold War.

I could not leave the base until I went to the company's orderly room to sign out on an off-post pass. My family walked with me to the company area; they were not allowed in the barracks as it was off-limits to family members. My family waited outside while I went into the barracks to change into something more comfortable and sign out for my pass. Leaving the company area, my family was waiting just outside. Then we walked to the parking lot where Dad had parked the vehicle.

Dad asked where I wanted to go for dinner. I told him it did not matter. While driving around, Dad headed toward the front gate and down the street toward Wrightstown where he spotted a nice family restaurant. Once inside, we caught up on things going on at home. It was only about eight weeks since I left home, and nothing had changed at the old homestead. My twin had a job, and he said it was in a textile mill about a one-half-hour drive from Waterville. That was the same manufacturing plant my dad worked at. We had a wonderful time at dinner and caught up on the current events at home.

After dinner, Dad drove us back to the barracks. We said our goodbyes, and then the family left for the hotel where they were staying. I returned to the barracks and signed back in. Then, I went to my bunk area and packed my belongings. I wanted to be ready in the morning to move to the holding barracks while waiting for my orders. I would relocate to Fort Polk, Louisiana, in the hot weather for jungle training.

After packing and taking an inventory, I headed to the service club. I would play Pinochle, and it was a fun game to play. Pinochle is a delightful card game—this is the service club where I learned to play the game. I asked around to see if anyone wanted to play a game of pinochle. It did not take long to get a foursome to play pinochle. We played for two hours, and then I left to return to the company area. Many of the men had already gone as their orders had arrived.

Morning came, and the first call rang out; the few of us formed a formation outside. There might have been about thirty of us there. Our platoon sergeant gave a little speech and told us to check the orderly room after breakfast to see if our orders came in. Now that basic training was over, things seemed a little slower. I had breakfast at the consolidated mess hall, which was much different from the company mess.

I returned to the company orderly room and saw my name on the list of orders. I picked up my orders and checked to see where I would go. Like others told me, it is Fort Polk, Louisiana, for jungle training. I could not figure out why I was going for jungle training.

The following day, I went to the C.Q.'s office and asked why I was going for jungle training. The captain told me everybody goes for jungle training. He said jungle training was advanced and that I would go to Germany. After hearing him, I felt better about wanting to go to Germany. This way, I could take leave to visit my pen-pal Gail in Bolton, England. I was on track for my plans to vacation in England to meet Gail as soon as time permitted.

Chapter Seven

Advanced Training Fort Polk, Louisiana

While waiting for a flight at the nearby Air Force Base next to Fort Dix, I met one of the soldiers stationed at Fort Dix training with me. His name was Thomas; unbelievably, his first name was Tom. He and I started talking about the training we had just finished. We talked about our families and all the everyday things ordinary people do. Thomas and I were both grateful that Basic Training was over. Thomas and I had orders for Advanced Infantry Training (AIT), which would be much more intense training. The next day, Thomas and I shared a cab to the Airport.

We had about an hour before our flight would leave from the Air Force Base. We sat at one of the local eateries to have a beer before boarding the plane. Sipping on our beers while sitting at an airport bar, we learned more about each other as we talked. Looking around from where we were, we noticed more soldiers arriving. We exited our seats, grabbed our carry-on bags, and headed to the boarding gate.

Thomas and I sat in the seating area, waiting for our flight to depart. There must have been about twenty troopers waiting for the same flight. We would fly on Trans World Airlines (TWA) with a one-stop Atlanta, GA. The flight would take just under two hours. Thomas and I had picked up something to snack on before we boarded the aircraft. From the PA system, we heard an announcement that our flight had arrived and was boarding at our gate.

While waiting for the doors to the flight gate to open, I ensured I had all my personal belongings with me. Within minutes, the doors opened, and some people coming off the airplane met their families and friends. Once all the departing passengers were off the plane, we waited for the call to start boarding. Thomas and I planned to sit together on the flight. We heard over the PA system that we should begin boarding the aircraft. Once Thomas and I entered the airplane, we headed halfway down the aisle and sat down. Thomas sat first next to the window, and then I sat in the aisle seat. After the passengers boarded the aircraft, the door closed, then the plane left the docking area.

The flight attendant collected our boarding passes once the airplane was in the air. After the steward had collected the boarding passes, I noticed open seats, so I moved to an empty row. I stretched across the row of seats and took a nap. Back in the '60s, airplanes hardly ever met their capacity.

Arriving in Atlanta, Georgia, we had to disembark the aircraft as we had a 3-hour hold-over. Thomas and I then waited for another flight to finish our trip to Alexandria, Louisiana. With a three-hour holdover here in Atlanta's airport, Thomas and I walked to one of the restaurants for food and a beer. In 1965, some States allowed eighteen-year-olds to drink alcohol. The first time I drank beer was while I was in basic training. So, being new to drinking, I limited myself to only two beers.

Both Thomas and I ordered a beer and a burger. The burgers were fifty cents each. A dollar went a long way back then. But of course, my first monthly paycheck was eighty-seven dollars. After eating and drinking, we paid for our lunch and left a twenty-five-cent tip for the waitperson.

Walking around the terminal since there was another hour before our flight would depart. Noticing a couple of phone booths, I called my parents to let them know I was doing okay during my transition to Fort Polk. I would also call again when I arrived at the base. After the phone call to my parents, I started walking through the terminal. I headed back to the departure gate area as it was approaching our departing time. Listening to the PA system announce my flight was boarding and getting ready for departure. When I boarded the plane, the flight pilot greeted everyone at the door. This time, Thomas and I each sat at a window seat. The door closed, and the aircraft left the docked area.

The aircraft taxied toward the main runway from where the plane would take off. Once in the air, the steward gave us the mandated instructions for an emergency. She said there was harsh weather ahead and that we should not worry. After the briefing, the steward came through the narrow aisle and collected our tickets.

We were on the flight for about fifteen minutes and flew into hazardous weather. The airplane started bouncing like we were riding on an old dirt road. Then, the lights in the cabin went off. We heard the pilot on the PA system telling us not to worry. All was fine; this was the norm during this kind of storm. After several minutes, the lights went on, and the flight returned to smooth flying.

Arriving at Alexandria Airport, we disembarked from the plane. More military personnel were getting off the plane with us. Thomas and I went outside the terminal and got into a cab on the curbside, waiting for fares.

The cab driver was a Black man. Before he started his taxi, he told us that one of us had to leave and take a different one. He explained that he was afraid for his life if he simultaneously took a white and a black fair in the cab. Wow, that was welcoming. Thomas gave me the cab, and he got out and waited for the next taxi. I showed the cab driver the address of my travel orders, and off we went. Once at the base, I paid the cab driver and thanked him. I waited for Thomas to arrive before reporting for duty. It was just minutes before Thomas got into the other cab. Thomas and I went to the arrival destination together. We went to our new training office location to report.

Advanced Individual Training had already started. We had not even unpacked our bags yet. We were in a formation in front of our barracks. The Drill Instructor had us count off in fours. The number we sounded off with would be the squad we would be in. I would be in the third squad; my bunk would be on the top, fourth from the Platoon sergeant's office/bedroom.

The bathroom was on the other end of the barracks. Like the barracks at Fort Dix, it had no stall dividers. There were a dozen toilets, and it was uncomfortable sitting and taking a dump with someone on the toilet so close to one another that we almost touched each other's elbows. Being in a Catholic religious home, learning this was not how a Christian should live.

Not every Christian like me likes displaying this manner in front of others. The showers were not any better; open gang showers, the Army put me in another uncomfortable way of life.

Many people did not like to take showers; one guy smelled severely. One night, someone suggested we should give this guy a GI shower. Some of the guys grabbed him, and others ripped off his clothes until he was completely naked. Once he was in the shower, some other guys started scrubbing every inch of his body. I swear some guys were enjoying their work. I thought these guys were having fun. I am glad I had no part in this action.

For the next few weeks, training was very vigorous and intense. While stationed here at Fort Polk, time went by quickly. There were many activities in the classroom and out on the ranges.

One Saturday evening, one of my new friends, Ken, and I had an off-post pass. We headed to a nearby town, Leesville, also known as Sleesville. Ken wanted to go to town to get a little lady action. Not long after getting on the bus, about 15 minutes, we arrived in Leesville. We went to a bar for a beer, and Ken looked around for a good-looking babe. I was still a virgin who was not interested in getting lady action because I feared getting VD (venereal disease) even though we were given condoms before leaving the post with our passes.

After a few beers, a young lady in her mid-twenties asked if she could sit with us. Ken did not even think twice about it and said sure. The girl looked incredibly beautiful. Ken asked what she wanted to drink, and she asked for Whisky and coke-cola. The three of us talked for a while; she was a working girl who tried to get down to business then and asked who would be the first to take her to bed.

I looked at the girl; as I mentioned, she was good-looking, friendly, and slim with a great-looking body. I told her I was not interested in having sex with her, but my friend was. She told us she had an apartment just minutes from the bar. Ken was ready and informed the girl that I would be coming with them as I would wait for him at the apartment. We walked to her place; it was a beautiful night for the short walk. Her apartment was on the ground floor. When we got into the apartment, there was a little boy in the room and an older girl about 15 years old. The girl was the babysitter. The girl we came with paid the sitter, then the babysitter left.

The young lady and Ken headed to the bedroom, and she asked me if I would watch the little boy while she was with Ken. I stayed with the boy and watched TV, but I was not paying attention to the little boy. Suddenly, I heard the boy yell at his mother outside the bedroom door. He yelled out, “Mommy, are you done yet?” I felt like crap, so I asked the kid what he wanted. He wanted water, so I got him some water.

As expected, Ken and the young lady came out about fifteen minutes later. I was getting ready to leave when the girl looked at me and asked if I had changed my mind. I smiled and said to her, "Thanks for the offer, but I am still uninterested." She gave me a little treat and flashed me just before we left; I have to say she did have beautiful, firm breasts. After leaving the apartment, we flagged down a cab and headed back to base. I returned to the barracks and headed straight to bed as I was tired.

The next four weeks went by in a flash. We did jungle training in the classroom, the ranges, and the forest. Let me tell you about this one time we were out in the forest and had to dig foxholes because we would spend the night in them. The foxholes we had dug were two men's foxholes. This guy I was with was full of questions I could not handle much longer. On a nearby two-way radio station, I heard that one of the leaders was looking for someone to go on a recon mission. Going on a recon mission gave me a reason to escape this guy. I answered the call and took off for the recon training mission.

I was gone for about an hour and a half. When I returned to find my foxhole. I noticed my partner was asleep; I flashed my light at him and saw a snake in the hole with him. I slowly woke up my partner so as not to disturb the snake. I signaled with a Shush and pointed to the snake. The snake might have been about 3 feet long. My partner saw the snake; he took off like a bat out of hell. One significant giant step, and he was gone out of the foxhole, not to be seen until morning. Later, he told me he had gone to the medical tent for the remainder of the night. He told them he was having nightmares and could not sleep.

Another graduation in a couple of days and then off on two weeks' leave to go home to Maine before leaving for Europe. I had just received my transfer orders for Friedberg, Germany 1st/36th Infantry. Most guys had orders for Vietnam, and my orders were for what I enlisted. In about four weeks, I was to report to the 3rd Armored Division in Frankfort, Germany. From there, I would travel to the unit I would have been assigned.

Chapter Eight

Starting Two Weeks Leave

A few weeks before graduating from Advanced Individual Training, I went to the American Express office in the same building as the post-exchange building on the base. This office also functioned as a travel agency. I had bought a plane ticket to return home to Maine, with a connecting flight to New York to board a ship bound to Bremerhaven, Germany. I received travel pay with my orders, but the travel pay was from the base to the New York Harbor. I had to pay the difference. On Saturday afternoon after graduation, I was on my way to the airport on the Army bus—a free ride. Flying on a TWA airline to Atlanta, then on to Boston. I would catch a flight to Waterville, Maine, from Boston on Northeast Airlines.

It has been nearly five months since I left home, and I am getting excited about going home on leave to be with my family and friends. The flight to Atlanta and onto Boston went without disruption or flaw. Landing at Logan Airport was on schedule; I had to change flights in Boston, giving me time to go to the men's room to freshen up and then get a bite to eat. After having something to eat, I walked over to the departing gate. Reading the flight time departures, I noticed the flight to Waterville would make one stop in Portland. Portland is about one hour and twenty minutes away from Waterville by car.

I heard the announcement on the PA system for boarding flights to Portland and Waterville, Maine. Bags in hand, I headed to the boarding area. About thirteen people were boarding this flight, not counting the crew, and this airplane was a 24-seater. The plane taxied to the runway, and then we went up, up, and away. This flight was noticeably short as the flight was only about a hundred miles as the crow flies. The air flight attendant had enough time to collect the tickets. This flight was over in less than an hour in the air.

The airplane arrived in Portland, Maine. Long enough to drop off passengers and pick up a couple headed to Waterville. This next flight would take about the same time as flying from Boston to Portland.

Sitting next to me on this flight was a young man traveling to Skowhegan State Fair, the oldest State Fair in Maine, about twenty miles from Waterville. Bobby R. was a famous singer; Bobby asked me if any cab company in Waterville would take him to the fairgrounds from the airport. I told him my dad might be able to take him to the fairgrounds.

Arriving in Waterville was exciting for both me and my family. As the plane stopped in front of the terminal, I looked out the small window and saw my family waiting. Mom, Dad, my twin brother Gil, and Linda (my sister) were there waiting to greet me. Dad grabbed my bags and put them in the car's trunk. Then, I introduced Bobby to my mom and dad. I asked my father if he could take Bob to the Skowhegan

State Fair. Without hesitation, my mother said Dad would be more than happy to drive him to the fairgrounds.

After dropping Bobby off at the State Fair, we headed back home to Waterville, and Mom asked me if I knew who Bobby was. I told her I had no idea. Mom said she saw him singing his songs on American Bandstand on TV; he was a recording artist.

On my first night home, I wanted to visit my friends. My mother was controlling; she wanted me to stay home with the family. I went to what was my room when I lived at home, and it was different. The bed was gone, and not only that, but all my stuff was also gone. I asked my dad what happened to all my stuff, and he said it was all in boxes in the basement. Mom did not take long to remove everything from my bedroom after I had left for Basic Training. It did not matter because I knew that once I left the Army, I wouldn't want to stay in the same house under her rules. I couldn't live with my mother.

On my first night at home, I went out with friends. One of my cousins called to see if I would go on a blind date with one of her friends. My cousin Margret showed up with her boyfriend. Then we took off and headed to Clinton, the friend's house. The girl she set me up with was pretty looking. We went into the house and met her parents; they seemed genuinely remarkable. After about an hour, we left to go to a drive-in movie. We stopped and picked up beers at a little market in Clinton. The film was at the local drive-in theater; I do not remember what the show was about. Even if I did, I would not have remembered it. We arrived at the drive-in movie and parked toward the rear of the parking area. My cousin's boyfriend and I went to the concession stand to get snacks to enjoy. The show began right after we arrived back in the car. It was not long before the car windows fogged up. I did not know this girl, but she was very friendly. After we drank a couple of beers, we made out with each other, kissing and caressing. She let me feel her up, but only over her clothes; she was not willing to allow me to go under the shirt. I was not the kind of guy to be aggressive toward girls.

The show ended at approximately 10:30, and we left the drive-in. It was about 11:00 PM when I entered the house; my parents were still watching the late show. I went into the kitchen to see if there was anything I could find to snack on, as I was hungry. Mom and Dad came into the kitchen when they heard me moving around. We talked about how things were going with me and my next assignment. We talked for about an hour, and then I got up and went to that little room where the bed was.

Getting to the bedroom, I emptied my duffel bag as I would be home for two weeks. Mom in the hallway asked how my night went; she stared at me when I told her who I was with that evening. She told me the girl I was with was a no-good whore, and I should not see her anymore.

I stopped Mom and told her that if she did not stop running my life, I had tickets to Boston and would leave immediately. She left the room, and my dad told her to mind her business. I finished unpacking and then went to bed as I had a day planned for the next morning.

It was about 0700 hours when I woke up. Nobody was in the bathroom, so I headed to do my morning duties: shower and shave. That took about half an hour. Dad worked the 1500 to 2300 hours second shift at a Textile Manufacturing plant in Augusta; he made Army Blankets at that textile mill. I asked if I could drive him to work and pick him up after work so I could use the car. He said there was no problem with that; Dad trusted me. In my last year in high school, I worked with him, putting up television antennas on Saturdays and earning a few extra bucks.

Sitting down to eat breakfast, Mom entered the kitchen and made herself a cup of instant coffee. She and I talked, and nothing came up about the night before. Mom asked me what I thought about visiting family members in Hartford, Connecticut. Sure, it would be fun, so I asked her when we would go to Hartford. She told me Dad would take some days off from the mill and not work on roofs on Saturday. So, we would leave on a Thursday and return on Sunday night.

Tuesday was upon us; it was the third day of my leave. I always loved going to Hartford and visiting my cousins, aunts, and uncles; I loved them all. Years ago, they lived next door to us when we lived on Greet Street in Waterville. During the '50s and '60s, many people from the Waterville area moved to Hartford to work at significant businesses and other jobs.

The guys from the band were going to play in an auditorium tonight. I asked if I could go with them, not because they needed a ride this time as in the past. One of the boys had a car now, and they were not looking to use me for a ride. I told them I would happily go with them and missed attending their dances. They told me they would return to pick me up at about 1700. It would take about one hour and fifteen minutes, and the show started at 1900, giving us a little over half an hour to set up. After the invitation to go with them to the auditorium, I told my dad things had changed, and I did not need the car. We left at precisely 1700 hours. We made one stop at a convenience store to get cold drinks. We arrived at the auditorium at about 1830 hours. It took a few minutes to set up.

Once the music started, the place started to become lively. When the people outside heard the music, they all came inside, and the hall filled with partiers. Brewer's high school was sponsoring this dance. At these dances in the auditorium, the girls always outnumbered the boys. At this dance, I did not have a problem getting dance partners.

In the era of the British Invasion in the mid-sixties, the band played songs from British groups. I had a noticeably short haircut because of the Army, so most girls knew a guy with short hair was a service member. At the time, a girl approached me and asked me to dance with her. The next dance was fast, and we had an exciting time dancing. When the dance was over, I thanked her and started to walk away when the band began to play a slow dance. The girl asked if I did not mind another dance. This girl was just a little taller than I was. She held me tight; her perfect, rounded breasts lay on my chest. She did turn me on, and this girl could tell.

I danced with different girls for most of the night. The band played their last song for the night at 2300, and now they packed up the car and headed back home. While driving back to Waterville, the guys and I talked and talked. The boys asked questions about why I wanted to join the Army.

Chapter Nine

Hartford

I woke up early this morning excited to visit my relatives in Hartford, Connecticut. I didn't sleep well. Departing Waterville in around 1000 hours would mean arriving in Hartford around 1500, providing light traffic flow.

We were leaving for our Hartford trip, just like in earlier years when Dad would always take us on a family vacation. The drive to Hartford went smoothly. Dad had allowed me to drive from home until we reached the Boston area since Interstate 95 was still under construction. Having my license for less than a year, Dad didn't think I could handle the heavy traffic.

On schedule, we arrived at Uncle John's home on Wethersfield Avenue in Hartford. My cousin Janette lived in the next house with her husband and three children. They were also at Uncle John's waiting for us to arrive at their home. We were greeted by both families when we arrived in Uncle John's driveway. All the hugs and handshakes were well deserved, as it was about a year since we were together. This handshaking was the first time some family members treated me as a man, not just a nephew. In those days, living in Hartford was nice and not as hectic as today. Cole Park was nearby and would be where we'd spend several hours. It was enjoyable at night; we'd go to the park to catch fireflies and put the flies in the jar, acting almost like a lantern.

After settling in at Uncle John's, we all wanted burgers and drinks from the burger joint. We were three families to feed, and we had to get some take-out food. Our family had five, Uncle John's family had five, and Cousin Janette's family had another five people. Dad, Uncle John, and I went to the burger joint about two miles from the house. We ordered fifty burgers and twenty orders of French fries, plus fifteen drinks. In those days, a hamburger was ten cents, and the fries were also ten cents each, as were the drinks. Feeding fifteen people for about sixty cents each was not bad at all. After getting back to the house, we enjoyed our lunch. The parents gathered in the living room, and all the cousins went outside. We must have stayed up until midnight. At that time, my cousin Janette and her family left to go to their home across the driveway.

The next day, the adults stayed home, catching up on a year of family news. My cousin Becky, the oldest of Uncle John's children, went for a walk with my brother Gil and me; Becky was three years younger than me. Becky had called one of her friends to come out walking with us. Becky's friend's name was Carlene, and she was a hot-looking girl, 16 years old, two years younger than me. Carlene did catch all my attention. I believe Carlene was the highlight of my trip. Carlene and I got along well. Gil was jealous because he told Mom I could not leave my hands off Carlene when we returned to the house.

That didn't stop me from returning to her the next day; Carlene and I walked to Cole Park and had a wonderful time. We held hands while walking to the park just a few blocks from the house. Being in the Army may have had something to do with Carlene wanting to be with me. I was good with her, even when I held her and kissed her on the lips. I did get her address so we could write to each other. Right, she never wrote to me. That was all right. I was not going to be around for at least four years. For the two days I was with her, I enjoyed her company.

One day, Gil and I wanted to visit the park with Janette's two daughters, Kate and Maryellen. They were 2 and 3 years younger than we were. So, we walked to the park and checked out the entire park. We swung on the swings and then tried some tennis for a while. After two hours, we headed back to their home for supper. Janette and her husband Del were our parents' age, and Janette was my cousin.

After supper, we all sat outdoors and talked mainly about myself and my plans while in the Army. I told them I hadn't had any idea what I'd do while in Germany. Germany was still rebuilding from World War II. I tried to get some information about Germany. Back in the sixties, we didn't have the technology we do today, so I didn't find much information about the Country where I'd be living for the next three years.

The next day was Sunday morning. We all got up early, had breakfast, and went to Sunday Mass at the nearby Church. We left to go home right after the Church Service. We headed out on Interstate 84 to the Mass Pike, and that took us to Interstate 95 going north through Boston. We arrived home around 1700 hours. I helped unload the car and put things away. Mom did not like a messy house; everything had a place, and she ensured everything was in its place.

I called some friends to see if they wanted to play at Foxy's pool hall on Silver Street in town. Two of the guys from the band said they'd enjoy some time at the pool hall; again, Dad let me use the car. Before going out, my mother asked me when I'd be back. I told her, "I didn't know," she said she wanted to talk as my time was getting short before I left for overseas. I told her I didn't want to talk if she would say to me how I should live my life. I was a man, and I would do what I wanted and not listen to or take advice from anybody. I told her I'd be home at about 2330 and then go to bed after a long day.

I got the car keys from Dad and drove off to pick up the guys. We went to the pool hall on Silver Street and played pool; there were five pool tables and two pinball machines. The hall was clouded with smoke as it seemed as if everybody there had a butt to their lips. We found a table that was not in use. I put a dime on the table and called, "Rack them up, Foxy." It cost a dime to play a game, and Foxy would rack up the balls when he was in the hall; his aid would rack up the balls when he was out.

We played till 2130 hours and then went for a late-night lunch at Parks Diner on Main Street before taking the boys home. I met a couple of my high school friends at dinner. We talked for a while, then the boys and I left. I got home at 2300 hours, just half an hour early, as I said I would. Dad and Mom were still up watching the late show on

TV. I gave Dad the keys and said thanks for using the car. I went to my bedroom, and that was it until the following day.

The next day, I went to the local shopping center to get a few things before heading to New York City to catch the troop ship carrier. This ship, by the name of General Gerard, carried troops to Germany during the Cold War. While at the plaza, I saw an old friend, Marilyn Massey. Marilyn was three years younger than I was to the day. That's right, and we shared the same birthday. She lived close to where I lived when I was in Junior High. Seeing Marilyn enter a department store, I followed her and saw her in the ladies' department. It may have been a couple of years since I've seen her. When we spoke, I could tell she wasn't interested, and that was it. I then left the store and went home.

Later that evening, after 2200 hours, I went to the Morning Sentinel to see the crew I worked with in the circulation department before entering the Army. It was nice to see the guys again. My old boss was named Ralph, and his aide was Alan. We all went into Ralph's office and chatted until the press started spitting out the newspapers. When midnight came, the crew took a half-hour break, and we all went to Parks Diner for coffee. The restaurant was on Main Street, and I went home when the team left the diner to return to work.

Before bed, I checked everything to ensure nothing was left behind. I did have my travel orders and pay records with me. The travel orders were given to me just before I left my last base, and I did not open the envelope as instructed. When I saw my brother Jeff while visiting him at his base in VA., he told me something about the pay records. He told me to open it carefully when I got them and not destroy the envelope. He told me to remove my pay record from the package for last month. I didn't have the nerve to do anything that dishonest.

Saturday had arrived, and this was the day I would be leaving for New York City. Before going down for breakfast, I packed my duffel bag and one suitcase I had bought to go to the World's Fair with Pete, a co-worker at the newspaper, and he and I made plans to visit the New York World Fair.

Chapter Ten

Crossing the Atlantic Ocean

My flight left in a few hours from Waterville Airport to Boston and then to New York City. After breakfast, Mom cleaned the kitchen and washed the dishes. Mom did not like a messy house. I did not leave anything behind, knowing I had forgotten anything in the room. Mom would throw it away as she did to all the stuff I had left behind when I left home in June.

Rose had already left for school, a sophomore at Waterville High School, and Gil had left for work. Mom, Dad, and I went to the airport. When arriving at the airport, the plane was already on the tarmac. I believe Dad must have taken the time to talk to Mom. About nagging me before leaving on the flight that would take me away from home for a long while. We exited the car, and Dad grabbed my bags from the trunk. Mom was getting too emotional as her eyes were watering up.

When I entered the terminal, I proceeded to the check-in counter to get my bags checked in. I only had a few minutes before I boarded the plane. We said our goodbyes. Hugs and kisses, I left the terminal and boarded the small plane. As the aircraft taxed off, I could still see my parents waving to me.

The flight would stop in Boston and then go on to New York. As this was a connecting flight, I wouldn't have to retrieve my bags when arriving at Boston International. It was a short flight to Boston, arriving in about half an hour. After retrieving my bags, I checked for the gate number from which I would depart. While approaching the boarding gate, I noticed other soldiers were waiting for the same flight. I checked the flight schedules on the TV monitors to see if the flight would be on time. With enough time to get a light snack before boarding the flight, there were a few places I could take the time and sit for a light lunch.

This flight would take about one hour once the plane is in the air. The plane might have been three-fourths filled with passengers; about 20 military troops were on this flight. With the Korean Conflict, the Vietnam War, and the Cold War, many soldiers from all military branches were traveling, crossing the world.

When arriving in New York and disembarking the plane, passengers headed to the baggage claim. Once I had retrieved my luggage, a couple of Army Officers met me and were looking for troops heading for Germany. One of the officers ordered us to go to a specific area to wait for the other soldiers arriving from different flights.

We left the terminal to wait for the military bus to take us to a troop transport. Once at the ship's loading area, I got ready to walk on the walkway into the belly of the vessel. I was required to show my travel orders. Once I arrived on the ship, I followed the command to go to the sleeping quarters, and this ship would depart on a ten-day journey to West Germany.

Remembering what my brother Jeff told me when arriving on the ship. Going to the bunks, I should take the top bunk because I wouldn't have to worry about getting vomited on me if someone were seasick. He suggested I put all my belongings on the bunk with me. I certainly did not want to find vomit in my shoes. I Placed all my stuff on the bunk, climbed onto the bunk, and fell asleep.

I woke up a few hours later, not seeing anyone in the bunk room. I left the area and found a staircase that would allow me up on the ship's deck; hundreds of troops were there. The troop carrier was moving out of the New York harbor and passing by the Statue of Liberty, which was beautiful. It was my first time seeing the Statue of Liberty in person. Another first for me was my first time on a ship that would be crossing the Atlantic Ocean. I was getting excited about going to Europe, and soon, I would go to England to see Gail. I had studied about Germany and wished I had learned more about Europe than just Germany.

Once on the open sea with no land in sight, we were all called out on deck for instructions on ship evacuations. Afterward, we were taken by groups and given a tour of the ship and the places we were allowed to go. There was a game room, movie theater, a library, and other areas of interest like the head (bathroom). Of course, the galley, also known to Army personnel as the mess hall.

After going through the ship's tour and returning to the bunk room, I jumped on the bunk to relax. It was tight on the bed, and my bags were at the foot of the bed. Ever since I can remember, I have had a trust issue. It was not easy for me to trust anyone. My bunk was about two feet from an I beam. After falling asleep again, what I thought would be a nap was a whole night's sleep.

The wake-up call was at 0600, and we did hear the sergeant in charge blow his whistle and walk through the bunk room. He was banging on anything he could to make loud sounds. I'm not sure how many bunk rooms there were on this ship. Knowing about three thousand troops were heading to Germany for assignment. The ship's crew were in another part that wasn't so crowded. Another group of travelers was the officers and their families, and they stayed in staterooms.

The showers were on the far end of the ship. The boat would go up and down from front to back when the waters were rough. The water from the showers would come out in spurts. We stayed in a very tight quarter; waiting in line to get to the showers was prompt. Five-minute showers were all we got, so that would be a quick shower.

After the first call, we all headed for the galley for breakfast. I noticed a lip on the edges of the tables so that when the ship started to rock, the food trays would not fall on the floor. Some of the troops were seasick and could not eat much; I was fine and did get to eat well. I might have gained weight on the ten-day trip across the Atlantic Ocean.

After breakfast, we were all to report to the duties assigned the day before. Some had kitchen police, and they were already on duty. Some of the troops had guard duty in the stairways, so unauthorized personnel would not go to parts of the ship that were off-limits to us troops in transit. While I was asleep in my bunk, I missed the assignment call. Everybody went to their assigned posts. Oh well, this would make my trip more like a vacation.

After everybody went to their duty stations, I had no special duties that would allow me to roam the areas. My adventure on this ship was to begin. I went up on deck; it was a nice, beautiful day with the sun shining. Watching off the ship's side, I spotted dolphins moving as fast as the ship. It was a warm and sunny day, and some of the troops off duty would have enjoyed taking off their shirts and lying in the sun. We were not to strip off our shirts because the government employed us. If we got sunburned and could not do our job, we'd have received an Article 15.

Going back inside the vessel to visit the library was my next choice. I wanted to see if I could get some information on current news; some newspapers and magazines took some of my time to read. I noticed a couple of open portholes. I wanted to see if I could look outside. I approached one of the portholes and looked outside, sticking my head out of the porthole, looking around, and looking upward to see if anybody else was doing the same. Sure enough, looking up, I could see someone else was doing the same as I was. We began to shout at each other; I acquired her name and what base her father would go to in Germany, but nowhere near I was heading for Frankfort.

Sometimes, the troops would get to the back of the ship where we could stand on a small open deck, letting us see the ocean as we moved swiftly through the waters. When the seas were rough, the ship would conquer some 30 to 40-foot waves. It seemed scary initially, but it didn't take long before we were used to the high ocean waves.

We all, 3,000 soldiers on this one level, were headed to Bremerhaven, Germany. With one stop in Southampton, England. On the eighth day we docked in England, the vessel had stopped in England for an entire day. I watched as numerous vehicles and other items were unloaded from the vessel's hull, assuming this vessel had multiple tasks.

While docked in Southampton, England, most of the troops tried to get to stay on the main deck as we wanted to see all of England as we could. People on the dock below would wave to us as we returned the welcoming waving.

With just one day on this ten-day voyage across the Atlantic Ocean, the ship would have to head east into the North Sea. The vessel would be leaving for the last leg of this trip, arriving at Bremerhaven, Germany. The preceding drill on this journey was in the middle of the night. All went well; an exercise like this would take about an hour and a half from start to end.

Once the drill was over, most troops started putting their belongings in their duffel bags and other carriers and going to the galley for our last meal on this trip. I did enjoy this trip; maybe it's because I was duty-free, just like a vacation.

I was getting excited about arriving in Germany. Entering the harbor in Bremerhaven, Germany, I was instructed on what to do and expect upon getting off the ship. Many people were watching the vessels coming into port. We were all called to prepare for the departure from the belly of the ship.

Once off the ship, we were bused to a train station and boarded a train for a trip to Frankfort, which would take two days to get there. The train would take this long to get to Frankfort because the US troops on the trains for military purposes would have the last resort for train movement. The train spent many hours at train yards or sidetracks while the regular German train traffic had priority.

The train car we were in was a sleeper car with four soldiers in each sleeper compartment. If you had the money and didn't care for the Army food, there was a lunch car on this train. Riding this train was the first time I had ever ridden on a train. I would enjoy the new way of life for the next three years.

Chapter Eleven

Arriving in Frankfurt

Arriving at the Frankfurt Hauptbahnhof, the train station in the city center was a sight to see. This train station has twenty-four rail tracks leading into the building under one roof. I was amazed by the remarkable architectural design involved in this station. The station has many markets; it appears to be a shopping mall.

I grabbed my bags off the train and walked toward the street. An Army bus was to take us to the replacement center a few blocks away.

Many troops assigned to Germany had to go through the 21st replacement center in Frankfurt.

Once at the replacement center, we formed a formation in front of the Company area. We were assigned a room, a bunk, and bedding for the bunks. This building would be where I would stay until I received an assignment. While at the center, I could not go outside the compound and into the city outside the gate. I spent time in the day room watching AFN TV, Armed Forces Network, and playing pool. Someone was always in the day room, so finding someone to play pool with wasn't tricky.

I was at the replacement center for three days before being called to the company office. After reporting to the orderly room, the company clerk gave me my orders for my next assignment. I would leave the following day for the 1/36th Infantry in Friedberg, about thirty-two kilometers from Frankfurt. I was expecting an Army bus to take me to Friedberg Barracks. Instead, I was picked by who would be my Platoon sergeant. After a brief interview, the sergeant took me to Battalion Headquarters to sign in with my orders. The sergeant took me to the infantry Charlie Company, where I would be for three years. I entered the orderly room and met First Sergeant Fields. He was from Bath, Maine, about fifty miles from my hometown.

Sergeant Dobbs, my platoon sergeant, walked me over to meet the squad members. All buildings on this post were built in the thirties as they housed German soldiers. Sergeant Dobbs and I left the orderly room and walked down the hall to my new room. Sergeant Dobbs would introduce me to the other squad colleagues, where I would be bunking.

The squad room had eight bunks, which was much better than having 44 bunks in one room and being assigned a vacant bottom bunk because someone had just rotated back to the States. I was near a window with a view of the company area. This room was much better than the barracks at Fort Dix or Fort Polk. I had my locker to keep my individual property locked up. Sergeant Dobbs mentioned that the team would be off duty at 1630 hours. As we left the room, he let me know I should make myself at home. I got settled in by putting away my items where they belonged. As he left the room, Sergeant Dobbs said he'd return at 1630 hours when the team returned from work.

After putting my things away, I took my empty suitcase to the storeroom to be stored until I needed it. While in the supply room, the clerk asked if I needed any locks for my footlocker and wall lockers. I gave him a yes, and he handed me two padlocks. I had to sign for the padlocks.

It was a while before my team would be back from work duty. I took a walk around the base to familiarize myself with the area. It would be lovely to know where the locations were: PX, snack bars, and coffee shops. The PX was near the front gate. The snack bar was in the same building as the PX but on the second floor. I also spotted a coffee shop near the motor pool. The coffee shop had coffee or soft drinks for ten cents a cup.

I was heading back to the barracks and checking out the day room. The day room was on the second floor, and I visited because there were plenty of things to do in the dayroom. There was a great service club not far from the barracks. I was returning to the squad room and waited for the team to arrive. Sergeant Dobbs was waiting for me. He told me the company was to have a formation. Then, the company would go to the motor pool for the daily communication check. If you are asking me if I would like to join them, no problem. I would love to go to the motor pool with the team.

We all marched to the motor pool for the daily communication check. Each squad was assigned a personnel carrier. The M113 personal carrier was our way of transporting the troops in the field. Being at the motor pool and meeting the team was a suitable time for me. Here are the names of the soldiers on my team: Layton, Victor, Willy, Breton, Morin, George, and King. These were to be my brothers while we shared the same room. Sergeant Downs was the squad leader. While at the motor pool, Sergeant Downs asked if I would sit with him later to discuss my new position with the United States Army.

I returned to the company area for the last formation of the day, and it went well, considering my first time with the company. Once dismissed from the company formation, some troops went to the mess hall for dinner. Some went into the barracks to clean up before eating.

I went to the squad room with a couple of guys. In the squad room, I saw Layton and Victor. They were the oldest squad members, about ten years older than me. Layton became my mentor; he was not the best choice, but he had been in the Army for almost ten years. With that thinking, he may have lots for me to learn. Later, I learned that Layton and Victor were drinking buddies, which may have negatively influenced me.

Later that evening, I saw Sergeant Downs in the orderly room; he was married and living off post. We talked about myself and my background. After a while, he asked what I would be interested in doing as a team member, and I told Sergeant Downs that I would do anything that would be helpful to the team. During the interview, he asked if I had a driver's license, and I answered yes. He then asked me if I wanted to be a driver as he heard Maine people knew how to drive in all types of weather. He told me drivers were exempt from Kitchen Police and Guard Duty. Not thinking too long, I told him I would gladly become the track driver. He went on to explain what my duties would be as a track driver. Sergeant Downs told me I could not visit the town for at least two weeks. When that happened, he suggested I go with one of the team members.

Dinner hours were from 1700 to 1800, and I headed out to the mess hall for dinner. There were great cooks in this company, and they had great food. After dinner, I would go to the squad room with the guys to see if the team had any plans that could include me. The guys were going to the EM (Enlisted Men) club for the evening. Many nights at the E.M. club, there would be live entertainment. This EM club was a particular club by a famous person; Elvis had built this club when he was stationed at Ray Barracks a few years earlier.

I saw the guys staying in their work clothes and getting ready to leave for the club around 2000 hours. Layton mentioned the club had no dress code, which meant I was just as prepared as they were. The club was about a five-minute walk from our barracks. The base wasn't large enough to have a cab or taxi.

Walking into the club was fantastic; the club looked like a large barn converted into this spacious club. Upon entering the club, on the right were some Slot Machines, something I had never played before. Once we sat at a table, the server came to the table and greeted Layton and Victor as if they were regulars. Layton ordered beers for the table at twenty-five cents a beer we could drink all night without making a hole in our pockets. Anne was the server's name; she may have been in her late thirties. Anne was on the heavy side; boy, did she have giant tits ever. Wow.

When Anne returned with the beers, Layton introduced me as a new team member. Anne had her way of welcoming newcomers to the club. I had no idea until Anne came behind me. She lifted her sweater and put it over my head. I almost came. She was not wearing a bra; those tits flapped against my face. I was very embarrassed; the guys at the table were gut laughing. And even people at other tables were aware of the happenings. I was raised as a strict Catholic and attacked by a big-boob lady, and this woman shamed me. Anne must have been about 20 years older than I was; that's over twice my age, making her an old lady. When Anne pulled her sweater back off my head, she looked at me and said welcome to Friedberg. Anne looked me straight in my eyes and said she had a fourteen-year-old daughter, and if I ever touched her, she would beat the shit out of me. She would be able to do it.

I'm not much of a beer drinker myself, and two beers were my limit. German beer is much stronger than beer in the States and very tasty. I left the table to go pee. I stopped by the slot machines on my return trip to check out the action. Watching the people playing the slots was enjoyable; I was not ready to lose money on the machines, even if they were only five-cent machines. I left and went back to the table with my team. That night, a live band from England was playing on stage. They were great; they reminded me of the nights in high school when the bands played dances.

On our way back to the barracks, we met up with Scott from another squad in our platoon. He stopped to talk with us. Scott was alone, walking in the opposite direction toward the EM club. Scott told us we were like brothers, but if we ever saw him downtown or in Frankfurt, he would not know us when he was with his kind and if we were in a fight. Scott told us not to get involved even though we worked together and would defensively fight against us. Back in the sixties, racial riots were happening back in the States. It wasn't only in the States but also in Germany, and It was among our military.

The following day, when I was in the company formation, I was introduced to the rest. There is no way I would ever remember all the people in this company. Let alone the hundreds or so of troops in the Battalion, which consisted of three companies and the Battalion personnel. The company commander dismissed the formation. I went out to the mess hall; there was a significant difference here in the mess hall compared to when we were in Stateside training. Here, there were no horizontal bars to go through before breakfast. We didn't have to wolf our meal in fifteen minutes at breakfast. Sergeant Downs stopped me before heading for the mess hall, and he wanted me to go with him after work formation.

After work formation, Sergeant Downs and I went to the motor pool to set me up for driver's training so I could drive a personnel carrier. I had to learn at least one hundred road signs, regulations, and driving information. At this time, Sergeant Downs left the area, which left me alone at the motor pool office training to become a track driver. I thought a little about the functions of the track. Then, I was given a license and returned to the barracks to see if Sergeant Downs was there.

It was Sergeant Downs's job to teach me about the personnel carrier. After lunch, we went to the motor pool, and he explained all I had to know about the track. Wow, I will operate a 24,000-pound Personal Carrier. He was a great teacher. Learning the ins and outs of the track did not take long. Sergeant Downs started the PC, and he was in the driver's seat, and I was the ground guide out of the motor pool. We went out back of the base where he would let me drive the beast. I loved it; I knew driving this giant machine was for me. After an hour of learning to drive, this track was fun for me. It wasn’t like driving a car; there was no steering wheel, only two sticks sticking from the floorboard.

We returned to the motor pool office after the short instructions on driving the track. Being set up for the track license, we had to sign a document saying I would be in charge and responsible for anything that could happen to the track.

When an alert sounded, my responsibility as the PC track driver would be to go down to the arms room where Ernest worked. He was the arms room person working to issue a 45-caliber revolver, rifle, and 50-caliber machine gun with a tripod. The 50 calibers with tripod weighed about 126 pounds. So, one of my team members would have to help me carry it to the motor pool. Then, mount it on the track at the track commander's hatch.

Every afternoon before our workday was over, all the units on base would have to go to the motor pool for track and radio communication checks. I'd have to start the track up to turn the radios on, and then I'd do a radio check with units from the Battalion command unit. When I had to get gas for the track, I would have to drive to the gas pumps near the wash racks. To do this, I would need a ground guard to walk in front of me until we were out of the motor pool area. At this time, everyone who walked me out of the motor pool area would climb onto the track and sit in the commander's seat with the open hatch.

Once at the gas pumps, I would top it off; the gas tank held 180 gallons (about the volume of a small refrigerator) of petrol. Most of the time, I would drive the track to the back of the base after topping it off and try to make a few U-turns on a dime with this 12-ton track. Running my PC on post gave me some practice in driving. I was nervous about our following alert, which was due very soon. Back to the motor pool to finish our daily work; we would call it quits for the day. Back at the barracks, after the day's work, the squad would meet in the squad room with the squad leader to critique our day's work. We talked about ways to make our workday better and more straightforward.

Around 2000 hours, we headed out to the EM club. A group of four women was playing at the club that night. Rounds for the table, I announced, maybe 6 of us there, so the beers would cost a total of $1.50, being only 25 cents a beer. Occasionally, we'd see a group from the States perform on stage at this club. When I saw Anne heading my way, I had to tell her I did not appreciate what she had done to me. We only stayed at the club watching the show for a few hours.

The flowing morning's first call was to get a head count to ensure all were present. After breakfast, we headed out to work formation. I was assigned to do the post-rubbish run. Someone had to do the job, and people wanted to go on the rubbish run for some reason. I went to the motor pool to sign out a two-and-a-half-ton truck for hulling the trash. I drove the truck, and the two other guys would hang on behind the vehicle, picking up the waste as we got to the dumpsters, and that was their job.

We headed out and went to each company in our Battalion for their trash. Picking up the garbage would take about two and a half hours. After picking up all the waste, we went to the base snack bar and had a light snack and a hot coffee. After our break, we had to bring the trash to the German trash dump. Once at the dump, the attendant stopped us. The attendant then advised me where I could park the truck for unloading. The German worker instructed us to leave the vehicle after parking the truck. He then told us we could go inside what looked like a break-shack. His comrades would unload the truck. We went inside the little hut. The person responsible greeted us. He followed us inside, telling us to sit down and enjoy a beer as he placed a case of flip-tops on the table. Now I understood why some guys wanted to go on the trash run. All the rubbish was disposed of by hand. If they found some stuff they could sell as used material, they would put it aside. Some things would be old magazines and any Army-related stuff they could sell at a used store. We were there for about an hour and a half until they had finished unloading the truck. I signed the paperwork, and we left the dumping area and headed back to the base.

Chapter Twelve

My first alert

At 0300 hours, the alarm for an alert sounded. There was no time to make up the beds when this happened in the middle of the night. I jumped into my clothes, quickly stopped at the restroom, and then headed to the arms room to grab my .45 handgun and M14 rifle. With Layton helping me, we took hold of the 50-caliber machine gun and made our way to the motor pool to get the track ready for the troops to load up inside the vehicle.

Once Layton and I mounted the 50-caliber machine, I made routine checks. I started the track, then engaged the engine, and dropped the rear ramp so the squad could take their positions. After starting the radios, I did the usual communications checks before Sergeant Downs arrived—he was always the last to show up since he lived off the post. Once the whole company was out and in the motor pool and in the vehicles, all track commanders gave the "all ready" signal. The company commander knew where we were heading but they never informed us what to expect. My track was about in the middle of our company convoy. My radio communication helmet connected me with the track commander. I sat in the small compartment with only my head sticking outside the track, just like Sergeant Downs, the track commander.

It was still dark, and we had to drive to the edge of the town. I'm sure the locals didn't appreciate it when we went out on alerts. All these vehicles making thunderous noises sounded like thunder roaring through the streets. It wasn't just our company on alert; the armored tank companies joined us. These alerts must have cost the US Government a lot of money. This brigade, the one I was part of, had a little over three thousand troops. Even the maintenance crew and the mess hall had to come out with us; sometimes, we'd be gone for up to three days.

Once out of town and on the open road, we could travel up to forty-five miles per hour (about sixty-five kilometers per hour.) It was fun at times; opening on the open road was much more challenging than the ten miles per hour limit we had on the post. Getting to our destination was more fun because we often had to drive off the road into the fields and forests. There'd be times when we'd have to make our roadways.

We sat at the wood line in the Fulda Gap area on the East-West German border. If fighting with the Russians broke out, this would be the area we'd be protecting and fighting in. The squad leaders would meet with the platoon leader, Captain Jones. Once the meetings were over, they would inform us what would take place.

Our mission on this alert was for our platoon, five tracks, and one jeep. The squad was assigned the lookout at a specific road intersection. The team would have to leave the track and settle in for a stay at this position. The team would have to set up and camouflage to avoid getting spotted. The mess truck would travel to our location so we could have something hot to eat. We'd be here for two nights and sometimes the day's last meal when the mess truck didn't show up. Sergeant Dobbs summoned the Squad Leaders together by radio. The captain let the Squad Leaders know that we could open a case of C-Rations, which was on board. That night, we ate C-rations dating back to WWII. Just thinking the food was at least 20 years old kind of made us think about the quality of the food, but some of it wasn't too bad.

Sergeant Downs asked a couple of guys to go on a recon mission. It was getting late, and nobody wanted to go. Layton volunteered to go, and I said I'd go with him. It was about 1900 hours; Layton, who had been to Vietnam twice, was a good person. I knew he would be a great teacher, and off we went through the woods and toward the village. We spotted some lights ahead, so we kept walking toward it and found it was a Gasthaus. Layton wanted to go to the Gasthaus, and I told him we were not supposed to do that while being on the field alert.

Layton told me he was going with or without me. So off Layton went. I wasn't far behind him, and we walked into the Gasthaus. The place went into complete silence. Layton and I walked up to the bar and tried ordering a beer. The proprietor would not sell us the beer because we had weapons and were on duty. Then we left and returned to the company area, except for one more stop. We stopped in front of a little market. I held on to Layton's weapons and helmet as he entered the market and came out with four flip tops. We then headed out back toward the track in the wooded area. Just before getting on the way,

Layton stopped and sat on a log. Then he flipped open a beer, handed it to me, and opened one for himself.

After drinking two beers each, we returned from our little scouting mission. I got back in the track and reported to Sergeant Downs. He let us find a place to sleep in the track. It was a tight squeeze for the night. Being the track driver, I could return to the driver's compartment and recline my seat. I got comfortable and fell asleep till the sunlight shone on my face, waking me up.

I woke up the rest of the crew. Sergeant Downs was called to a platoon meeting while waiting for the mess truck. Upon his return, he assembled the squad to inform us that the mess truck would be arriving to serve us breakfast. He also told us the alert was over, and we'd return to Friedberg after breakfast. That wasn't bad; there was only one night out this time.

While waiting for the mess truck to arrive, we had to ensure everything was how it was when we arrived at this location. We did have a small fire going so that whoever wanted could heat some water for washing and shaving. It wasn't too long before the mess truck showed up. After breakfast, we ensured we had all our equipment on board, started the engine, and waited for my turn to leave on command.

Being eighteen and driving this 12-ton track gave me a sense of responsibility. I received orders to move. I put the vehicle in gear, and off we went. We'd see young children waving their hands toward us, begging for food while driving through some small villages. The children expected a donation, and we'd break out a case of C-rations and hand them out as I moved slowly, not to scare any children.

Once back on base, we convoyed back to the motor pool. Once on base, I could not move until I had a ground guide. A few team members returned the 50-caliber machine gun to the arms room. As the PC driver, I cleaned the track. I cleaned the track inside, both inside and out then drove it to the wash rack for a thorough cleaning. Being a driver is another reason I was exempt from some duties.

After washing and cleaning the track, it was my job to go to the arms room and clean the 50-caliber machine gun. We skipped the previous communication checks in the motor pool as we came in from the field. Most of us headed for the showers to clean up and ate dinner at our mess hall. After dinner, a few of us went to the EM club after we were all cleaned up and everything was in its place. Another night of beer drinking, and then the rest was history.

Chapter Thirteen
Berchtesgaden

First, call on Monday morning. The company commander had an announcement he was going to make. It would be a reward for some of the troops. After the roll call, the captain announced it to the company. The company commander revealed that one person from each platoon would receive a week of R&R (Rest and Recuperation), sending some lucky soldiers to the General Walker Resort Hotel in the German Alps. The method he was going to use was to place every soldier's name into a hat and draw names. Specialist Rhea, Specialist Spooner, Private Jones, and Sergeant Smith were selected. From the names to receive the R&R leave. Finally, the last name drawn was mine. I told the company commander I didn't deserve the R&R as I had been there only a few months. The Commander told me to have a good R&R.

Rhea and I crossed the Atlantic on the same ship and arrived at the company at the same time. Rhea and I didn't realize we were on the same boat until we talked one evening at the EM club. The R&R leave would be to Berchtesgaden, which was about 550 km (about the length of New York State) away. We were also given $100.00 for the five-day leave. The leave would begin on the following Monday morning.

The following Monday morning, the five of us were picked up in front of the barracks by an Army bus to take us to the train station in town. We traveled from Friedberg to Frankfurt, then changed trains traveling to Berchtesgaden. The train ride would take most of the day, about five hours. There was about an hour and a half before our connecting train would leave the platform. Seeing the train arriving, we headed toward the loading platform. This time, all five of us were in the same compartment. We were on this train for over five hours. We got to know each other better beyond just being soldiers in the U.S. Army. There were stops in Wurzburg, Nuremberg, Munich, and Berchtesgaden.

The resort Hotel was in the Alps, and the United States government operated it. It was just a couple of miles away from the train station; a bus at the station was waiting to take us to the hotel. Our drive to the hotel was just spectacular, with incredible scenery. After getting off the bus, I retrieved my travel bag. Then, I set it down near the main entrance to the General Walker Hotel. Rhea and I took a few minutes to walk around the area, taking in the breathtaking scenery and snapping some pictures. Getting back to our bags, we entered the Hotel and checked in. I paid in advance for the hotel room, which was fifty cents a night. Rhea and I shared the same bedroom. There was no bathroom nor a shower in our room. The toilets and showers were at the end of the hallway. Overlooking the Alps was breathtaking, mountains as I'd never seen before.

After unpacking and settling into the hotel room, Rhea and I went to the front desk, asking which the least expensive way was to get back into Berchtesgaden. The clerk at the front desk told us if we walked a click down the road, we could locate a cable car that would take us to

Berchtesgaden. Riding the cable car would cost 50 pfennigs, about thirteen cents. Layton and I went back to our rooms.

When Rhea and I went outside to look around, lounge chairs overlooked the spacious scenery. Rhea and I sat down, just amazed at the view. A few minutes after we sat down, Jones asked what we had planned. We told him about our plans to head to town by cable car, which we were to walk a click six-tenths of a mile. So off we went and started walking toward the Cable car. There was a Gasthaus (Guest House) with inviting outside seating just before the cable car platform.

We decided to sit at one of the tables and order a beer. A young German girl came to our table and asked what we wanted. We each ordered a one-liter glass of good old tap German Beer. It was a beautiful sunny day; we couldn't have asked for better weather for being on this R&R leave. The girl waitress returned to see if we wanted anything else. We said we were happy with our beer. I asked the young girl if she would take pictures with us. At first, she didn't want a photo taken with us. We had finished our beer and asked how much it was for the beer. Two Marks was her answer. So, we all placed two marks on the table; she took 2 Marks off the table, thanked us, and then started to leave. We got her attention, and she then returned to the table. I told her we all wanted to pay. She told us it was 2 Marks for all three beers. That was about fifty cents in total. I told her she was such a great server that she could take the rest of the money as a tip. She thanked us repeatedly and then let us take a picture with her.

We got up from the table and headed to the cable car, large enough to seat four people. We went down the mountain; it was a beautiful sight going down. We could see some wildlife on the way down. I tried to take some pictures, but my camera wasn't the greatest of cameras. I had a 110 Instamatic Camera. I took a few photos going down. I saw a deer and took pictures, but the deer was hard to see because of the distance and the vegetation.

Arriving at the bottom of this mountain, we left the cable car and went right onto the village street. I walked to the ticket counter. I was checking to see when the last run up the mountain would be so we wouldn't have to take the bus or walk back. Riding the cable car took much less time to get to the hotel. Even with the one-k walk, it was a straight line compared to the winding roadway through the Alps.

Walking through what seemed to be a tourist town was very relaxing. It was like going back in time on Cobblestone Streets. The Streets were very narrow and surrounded by old buildings. I thought I would be returning to this place in the distant future.

Berchtesgaden, Germany

A river flowed through the little village of Berchtesgaden; the water looked clear as if it was coming from the mountain. The Alps still had snow on the higher parts of them. I noticed some people transported by horse and wagon. Groups of people sat on the grass in the parks; many sat at the sidewalk cafes, enjoying themselves in this beautiful, picturesque tourist village.

We noticed some empty chairs at one of the sidewalk cafes. We decided to sit down, have a couple more beers, and enjoy the site. We were hoping to meet some girls. Being the youngest of the group, I was hoping to meet a girl my age. Maybe around 18 or 19 years old. I never thought I'd have time to enjoy myself like this while in the Army.

About an hour had passed, and we drank a couple of beers. We left and headed to a local Gasthaus for good German food. We walked into what looked like a cozy Gasthaus with wooden floors, tables, and chairs. The inside of the Gasthaus looked like a picture taken two hundred years ago, nothing like what you'd see in the States.

A waiter greeted us warmly as we sat at a nearby table. He handed us menus, and the waiter took our drink orders. We ordered from the menu by pointing to the pictures of food displayed on the wall next to the kitchen. On the other end of the restaurant were some people who were going to play some old German music. The pleasant, relaxed atmosphere; we couldn't have asked for a better place to eat that afternoon.

When we finished our dinner and beers, we paid as we left the building, then headed toward the cable car. We took our time taking in all the sights we could on this once-in-a-lifetime trip at the Army's expense. Many people were getting off the cable cars. A few people were waiting to get on the cable cars to head up the mountain. Within a few minutes, it was our turn to get in the cable car. We didn't go all the way up the mountain. Our stop was about halfway up the mountain to the Hotel.

When we arrived back at the hotel, we stopped for the day. This hotel had no television sets, and some entertainment was in the lobby. The US Government operated the hotel for R&R leaves for the troops involved in the Cold War. For fifty cents a night lodging, this was one of the better Hotels I stayed in for the three years I lived in Germany, memories I'll never forget. That's why I'm writing about it today.

Getting ready to end the night and making plans for the next day, I stopped at the front desk and picked up some fliers and brochures to find something to do while we were in the southern part of Germany. I found a place I thought would be interesting to visit. Rhea and I decided to get the other three guys to go with us the next day. Rhea and I went to their rooms on a different floor and talked about the next day's trip to the Austrian salt mines. The five of us agreed that it would be a lot of fun and indeed there was something different we could do. The brochure gave us the schedule for the bus leaving the Hotel. A bus would depart from the Hotel at 1000 hours at no cost as it was an Army bus.

Chapter Fourteen
Berchtesgaden Continued
The Trip to The Salt Mines

Waking up early the following morning, I headed out to shower; as I mentioned, the shower room was at the end of the hallway. When I returned to the room, Rhea went for his turn in the shower. Rhea was gone for about fifteen minutes, and then I heard a knock on the door. It was Rhea—he had not taken a key room with him and was standing in the hallway without any clothes on. I opened the door, and he rushed in quickly, saying he hoped nobody had seen him. Rhea hadn't taken a towel because he thought they were provided in the shower room. Rhea told me he didn't want to put his dirty clothes back on after he had cleaned up.

As planned, we met the others from our group in the breakfast room and quickly ate a full breakfast. Some guests in the breakfast room were looking our way, and Rhea and I had an idea why. Some were even pointing, thinking it was funny. I looked back at them with a smile. Some of those people must have seen Rhea running down the hall naked. Rhea's face turned beet red; I told Rhea not to worry about it as we would likely never see these people again.

After finishing our breakfast, we had to wait for the bus to arrive, so we went outside to sit on the patio and enjoy the view, which again was spectacular. I lit a cigarette as I sat in one of the lounge chairs. The others, except for Rhea, lit up. Rhea didn't smoke, which was surprising because he was a tobacco farmer in Tennessee. We couldn't have asked for a better day. We would have another sunny day on this excellent vacation adventure to the salt mines inside the Alps.

The bus was arriving, so we put our cigarettes out and walked toward the bus. It looked like the bus would be full. As mentioned, the United States government ran this hotel for R&R leaves for the troops involved in the Cold War. There were probably 45 people getting on the bus. We were all Americans on this tour. I could tell because the children on the bus spoke English. While on the bus, I met an Officer, his wife, and their three children.

The ride to the mines wasn't very long. Within the hour, we arrived at the mines. Upon arrival, a tour guide met us as we got off the bus. The tour guide had us walk to an area just outside a small building. The tour guide explained to us what we were to expect and what to watch out for as it was for safety reasons.

We entered the building and walked toward an opening that led the group into a cave. We walked through the shelter for a short distance and then came to an ample space where we all gathered. The guide informed us we'd be going down a thirty-foot banister slide. At this point, we watched a short film showing us how to get on the rail and hold on to each other. After the movie, we walked to the banister slide. Before getting on, we were handed a leather mat with a belt attached to it. We put it on for our protection, as seen in the film we had watched. Sliding on a thirty-foot-long banister gets pretty hot on the backside. With this leather mat, we'd sit on it for the ride down.

Getting on the rail was easy: the first person would get on, followed by the second, and so on. We hugged the person in front by wrapping our arms around their waist and getting as close to the person in front of them, like spooning. When I got on the banister slide, I might have been the tenth person in line, ready for the descent. The person behind me was a WAC (Woman's Army Corp). When she got on behind me, she moved up to me until our bodies touched. I could feel her body-hugging my back, and I didn't mind it. While waiting for the rest of the group to get on, we got to know each other's names. I hugged Marilyn's body, the person in front of me, so you couldn't even pass a sheet of paper between us. My hands were locked together at the fingers and around her waist. Never in my whole life have I thought I would be between two beautiful women.

Once the whole group was on the rail, the tour guide instructed us to shimmy forward until gravity pulled us down the thirty-foot slide. Here we went; we were all tight together, and the trip down might have been about twenty seconds long. Once we arrived at the end of the slide, we had to quickly walk away from the rail's future, as the video instructed, so the people behind us could also get off the railing safely.

The slide down wasn't all that bad. We walked a little further into the cave as the tour guide spoke about the salt mine; the cave was very well-lit. I listened to the tour guide as we moved along the path to the next large opening. Still wearing our leather mats around our waist, we arrived at another banister slide. This one was 80 feet long. The process would be the same as the first slide: trying to get in line behind the lady in front of me on the first slide. My plan didn't work, but I didn't want to sit behind or in front of another man. That would be simply weird. I did manage to get in between females again for this second slide. At 18 years old, getting between two girls on this banister ride was exciting—definitely something I could write about someday.

I was seated and waited to get the instruction from the guide to start to shimmy forward until enough people were on the slope of the railing. A different girl was behind me, and her body felt friendly against my back. I could feel her body pushing against me. I did the same to the person ahead of me, and it was the thrill of riding down this 80-foot banister slide. I believe the lady in front of me could tell I was getting excited when feeling her push back on me. Then suddenly, gravity started to pull us forward down the 80-foot slide. This time when we arrived at the bottom of the drop, we did a little dancing jig as our butts got a little warm on the decline as the friction moved under us.

After we settled down a bit, the guide told us there was one more slide, this one 130 feet long. Oh boy, another drop; I wondered how far we were in the mountain now. We did the slide, and it got warmer than before. And, of course, we did a little dancing when we stopped after 130 feet of friction. We were now allowed to remove the leather pads we were wearing. At this landing, we approached a massive opening in the mountain and a museum for us to enjoy: a place to sit and a little souvenir shop. Surprisingly, there was what looked like a small lake in this cave; that's how significant this opening was. We were given a museum tour and watched a short documentary about the occurrence of salt in the past. I bought a souvenir at the shop. Once we finished at this location, the guide took us on a boat on this small lake to get across and continue our tour. On the other side of the lake were some small railroad tracks. The guide informed us we were to go onto these small trolley cars, which looked like small coal cars, and we were not to stand up when the vehicles were moving as there was low clearance.

After a 5-minute ride on the small salt car, we emerged from the mountain and into the daylight. We headed toward the bus, which was waiting for us. Once seated on the bus, the bus driver drove us back to the hotel. When we arrived back in Berchtesgaden, some people on board wanted to stop at the town square. When the bus stopped in the village, Rhea and I also walked off the bus to go to one of the local Gasthaus for a beer.

After we left the market, we headed toward the cable car lift, looking for a place to have dinner. The streets were narrow and paved with cobblestones. Rhea reminded me about the small Gasthaus we had stopped near the cable car stop earlier in the week. We decided to take the cable car up the mountain and stop at the Gasthaus for dinner. It was still light out, and sitting in the open air would be highly comfortable enjoying our dinner. We were not the only ones who had that idea. At least a dozen people were sitting outside, having dinner or waiting to be served. Looking around to find a place to sit, I saw the couple we had met in the salt mine, the lady who sat before me, which excited me. The couple motioned for Rhea and me to join them at their table.

We gladly accepted their invitation and sat at the table with them. The waitress brought each of us a beer after our newly made friends motioned to the waitress to serve us beer. We talked with each other, and we found out the couple was from Florida. Rick and Martha were friendly, finding out he had been in the Army for several years and stationed in Stuttgart. We had dinner and had a great time with our newly-made friends. It was an enjoyable evening as we didn't discuss our rank. After our meal, we parted ways with our newly made friends and returned to the General Walker Hotel.

As time passed quickly, our R&R leave was coming to an end. The next day, the last of our R&R leave, Rhea, Jones, and I took another day trip the hotel sponsored. The trip was to visit some of the not-so-famous places where Hitler hid during the war's end in the mountains. The bus left after breakfast, and only three of us went on this trip. The other two decided to attend another activity sponsored by the hotel. When we arrived at Eagles Nest, the bus stopped us at the reception center. A tour guide accompanied us for a walk around the grounds. The guide explained the different objects around the region. There were parts of bombed areas and other destructive items. Some areas had places we were not allowed. We entered a small building that led us to a tunnel into the mountain. We witnessed the detention locations where prisoners from WWII were held in these tunnels.

We saw holes in the bullet walls, remnants of those used to kill many prisoners of that time. This one tunnel Hitler's prisoners built during the war to make his escape into Austria. It took one thousand men one month of work around the clock to build that tunnel. Once back out of the belly of this mountain, walk back to the starting point. We saw many craters because of the bombing during World War Two. When returning to Berchtesgaden again, the bus driver stopped us off in town.

We stopped again at the same place as the day before for dinner. We'd also got to meet some of the locals. After eating some lunch, we wanted to plan for our last night on our R&R leave. So, we headed back to the hotel by cable car. Once at the hotel, we sat in the yard overlooking the Alps. Rhea went inside the hotel lobby to get some fliers so we could find something to do that night. We saw there were a lot of things to do in Salzburg, Austria. We had decided to spend some of the last few hours in Austria.

We cleaned up and changed into clean clothes. We were heading toward the cable car to get back into town to see if we could catch a bus to Salzburg. Upon arriving at the bus station, the ticket master advised us he would not take us across the Country's Borders. We tried another way: to get a cab driver to take us to Austria. We talked to the driver and asked him about possibly taking us to Salzburg for the evening. We had to make a deal with the driver. The cab driver said he would do it if he could wait there and bring us back. The cab driver wanted to get paid while he waited. We agreed; he wanted to check our military ID cards to ensure they could pass at the border.

The three of us jumped into the cab, and off we went. It was a twenty-five-mile ride, and because of the mountains, it took nearly an hour to get to Salzburg. We arrived at approximately 2100 hours; the driver stopped the cab in a well-lit parking lot and told us that he would be there until we returned—the fare cost us approximately $15.00 each, which we thought was fair. We went to a disco club; in the sixties, discos were big.

It was a little after 0100 hours, and we wanted to go somewhere to eat before heading back to Germany. Heading to where the cab was parked, we noticed a small Gasthaus. The lights were still on, so we saw people inside as we approached the Gasthaus. We entered the building and went to sit at the bar, where the bartender asked what we wanted. All three of us sat on the bar stools. No sooner than we sat down, we all simultaneously said beer. The bartender introduced himself as Karl; we exchanged names as we told him our names.

He knew we were US soldiers by the way we looked and, indeed, from our speaking English. Karl went on to tell us he was a driver for the United States Army during the War. Karl opened his wallet, took a small, folded piece of paper, and showed us a license he needed to drive a bus for the US Army during WWII. Karl asked us if we wanted something to eat. I asked Karl if he was still serving meals. Karl said no, but his wife would come down to cook us something. I mentioned we had a cab driver with us and wanted to know if he would feed him. Karl said no problem, so I went outside, asked our driver if he was hungry, and wanted something to eat. The cab driver returned to the Gasthaus with me. The meal was ready within an hour. His wife had made some Wiener Schnitzel with potatoes and some veggies. The meal was great, and the bartender talked our ears off. He told us he was thrilled we had stopped by his place of business.

As we were getting ready to leave and return to the hotel, Rhea asked Karl how much we owed him for the meal. He waved his hands and said it was his and the wife's pleasure to have us visit his home. He didn't want us to pay for the meal. We thanked them and shook his hand; his wife hugged us all. Karl said next time we were back in the area, we should come back to see him. We left the Gasthaus, headed to the cab, and returned to the hotel. You can see what a night we had and a night never to forget.

We arrived back at the hotel at about 0330 hours, giving us a couple of hours. Our bus would leave at 0800 hours, giving us about three to four hours of sleep. The wake-up call came at 0630 hours. We did some fast-moving to get a coffee before leaving on the bus to the train station. Arriving at the train station, we boarded the train and had a compartment to ourselves. Once the train pulled out of the station, we crashed and got some much-needed sleep.

The train stopped in Munich, and we had to make a train change this time. We disembarked the train and walked down the platform with our bags. The five of us gathered and talked about what we could do for an hour and a half before our next train left. Finding a station locker to place our bags in wasn't too tricky as there were everywhere. This train station was much larger than the one we had just left in Berchtesgaden but not as large as the one in Frankfurt.

We walked outside the station and headed toward Sonnen Strasse, just outside the München-Haupt Bahnhof (The Main Train Station). We walked a little, but Spooner and Sergeant Smith decided to stay at the station with plenty to do. Sitting at an outside pub, we ordered a sandwich and, of course, a beer. We were still in sight of the Haupt

Bahnhof. One of our favorite pastimes was watching people walking by. Some homeless people are sidewalk performers who like to walk by and beg for spare change, just like in New York City.

While enjoying our beer, a passerby stopped and asked if she could sit with us and buy us a beer. We didn't mind her sitting with us. Jones ordered a beer. She was an older lady, maybe in her thirties. We didn't expect her to ask Jones to go home with her, but she asked him. We all looked at each other and smiled. Jones turned her down and told her we were in transit on our way to Frankfurt. We finished drinking our beer and finished our sandwich. Then Jones told the girl we had to leave as our train was leaving in a few minutes. We got up, and the girl got up with us; she was beautiful and hugged us as we started to go. We had to be careful that she would not pickpocket us while giving us hugs. A hug from her was warm; she didn't have a bra on, which made the hug even warmer.

Getting back to the other two guys, we had a few minutes to wait for the train. Trains in Germany were always on time; we could set our watches on the station's time. Boarding the train, we had seats in a compartment, and all five of us entered this one compartment. We did have one more stop on the way. It would be in Stuttgart, with only about a twenty-minute holdover to change trains.

We were finally arriving back in Frankfurt, and with a quick train transfer to return to Friedberg, our vacation would end. We all agreed we had a great time.

Chapter Fifteen
A regular day 1/36th Infantry

Back to my regular workday in Friedberg. Monday morning wake-up call at 0600 hours, with everyone rushing to get cleaned up before breakfast. I hit the bathroom for my morning duties, shaved, and then showered. I returned to the squad room to make my bed and clean my area of responsibility: cleaning half of the hallway, sweeping the floor, and doing a quick mop-up job. The initial training took place at 0700 hours, and a roll call to ensure everyone was present. Being dismissed for breakfast, some troops headed straight to the mess hall while others returned to the barracks to finish cleaning. As for me, I went to the mess hall for a good breakfast, and most of the time, the food was surprisingly good.

My daily duty involved going to the motor pool to pull maintenance on my truck. There was always something to do to keep the track in good running condition. I'd first start the PC to warm up the engine and oil before checking all the oil levels. Sometimes, I'd need to change the track pads. When I changed track pads, I'd get help from some other driver. In exchange, I'd help them change their track pads when needed. We were military brothers; we helped each other.

The next formation was for work duty, and we were ordered to a specific task with no motor pool duties that day. This morning, I was assigned the rubbish run for the second time. The rubbish run lasted just a few hours—about 5 hours. Going with me was a driver and his two-and-a-half-ton truck, along with two other people to pick up the trash. After being dismissed, the four of us headed to the motor pool to pick up a vehicle. We had about ten places to pick up trash; each company had a rubbish bin, and each mess hall had a rubbish bin.

Once we finished at the dump, we returned to the barracks for lunchtime. Arriving at the company area, I released the two troops who picked up the trash. Then, the driver and I went to the wash rack to clean the truck. It didn't take long to wash the truck and return it to the motor pool. Walking back to the company area, I went to the orderly room to let the clerk know we had finished the rubbish run. Sergeant Bundy, my platoon sergeant, was in the tiny room by the office and asked how the rubbish run went.

Having had beer on my breath, I didn't want to get too close to Sergeant Bundy. I stayed in the doorway to talk to him. I told him everything went well and that the crew had done an excellent job. Surprised, the Sergeant looked at me and asked how the beer was. He saw the expression on my face and then told me he knew about the beer fest at the dump. Sergeant Bundy then informed me about what was happening at the village dump, and the C.O. didn't have an issue with it as the troops didn't get carried away and drink too much.

Then Sergeant Bundy followed me to the squad room and asked me what I would do after lunch. I intended to go to the motor pool, check out my track to see if it needed light maintenance, and then drive the PC to top it off with gas. After that, I was going to the wash racks to wash the truck. I took care of this track like it was my own.

Sergeant Bundy and I headed to the mess hall as we didn't want to miss all that good army food. NCOs did not sit with the enlistees. That's the way it was in the Army. After lunch, I returned to my room to wait for the afternoon formation. The company formation was the mail call. I was waiting for a package from home as my mother was supposed to send me a food package. While in the room with the rest of the Squad waiting for afternoon work, Sergeant Downs walked in with a personal announcement. Sergeant Downs invited the whole squad over for Thanksgiving dinner, which would be on the following Saturday.

After work formation, I headed out to the motor pool as planned. Layton and Victor came along with me to see if I needed help on the track. I could always use help when it comes to the track. Getting to the motor pool, I went to my PC and unlocked the driver's hatch. I climbed into it and started it up so I could have the power to drop down the back ramp of the track.

We removed everything from the track and ensured everything was clean and combat-ready. Once we finished cleaning the track, I started the track, with a ground guide, I drove out of the motor pool, and Layton was my ground guide. Once out of the motor pool, I stopped to allow Layton to board the track and get into the TC's (track commander) seat. I drove it toward the wash rack, where a long, wide, hard-top surface headed out to the back gate, barely ever used. The back gate was where we were allowed to drive the track and make split-second maneuvers. I opened it up and did about thirty-five miles per hour, and I would lock one lateral. I would lock up either the right or left track, and the track would make 180 degrees spin on a dime. After doing this a few times, I drove it to the wash rack for good washing. Layton helped me wash the track. Once done, I went to the gas pumps to top it off, then back to the motor pool.

After getting back to the motor pool, Layton and I had about half an hour before we had a radio check at 1630 hours. Nearly half an hour before the radio check, we headed to the snack bar for a coffee and a pastry. With enough time after our little break, we headed back to the company for the radio check company formation. After the company formation, we headed out to the motor pool for the final duty for the day. We marched out to the motor pool as a company.

After the radio checks in the motor pool were complete, we returned to the barracks to prepare for the day's last meal. After dinner, at about 1800 hours, some guys sometimes went to the athletic field to play some soccer with some locals. We were not allowed to play with the German population on the post, but we did anyway. We always had a fun time playing soccer with the local Germans. This one time, one of the German players fell and got hurt. One boy dislocated his wrist, and it didn't look good. After talking about what we would do, we all decided to send the Germans over the fence off the military base. The German boys who played soccer with us were not supposed to be on the post as they did not have the proper authority to do so. We had never seen these boys again, and mum was the word. We didn't report this soccer game and never invited them over again. Given this event, we would have received article 15 and maybe some time in the stockade.

After the soccer game, some of us headed back to the barracks. Some platoon members wanted to go to the Bahnhof bar in town. It was one of our favorite places to go off-post. It would take us about 20 minutes to walk to the Bahnhof bar. About 6 of us went to this bar. Layton and Victor were a little older than most of the platoon members. Their age is why some of us viewed them as wiser, but we were wrong.

When going downtown Friedberg, we were banned from wearing military clothing unless we were out on Army business. Once at the bar, we were known as regulars, which meant we always sat at the same table. Some regular Germans would ask us to play Foosball, and the Germans were damn good at this game. When we played Foosball, it would be for beers; the losers would pay for a round of beers. We didn't win often, but we did a lot of drinking. It took a while, but we did become surprisingly good at playing the game.

We were out on a day pass and had to return to the barracks before midnight. If not, we would have to enter the front gate because the back gate would be locked. If we didn't return by midnight, we would lose our pass privilege for a week. The AWOL (Absent Without Leave) was at an exceedingly high rate. AWOLs didn't look particularly good on the morning reports. After a while, the Brigade changed its rules as the day passed. Overnight passes were issued instead of day passes. AWOL just about disappeared from the morning reports.

It was about 2315 hours when we left the Bahnhof bar as we were still on the midnight curfew. We checked in at the orderly room on time—another momentous day. I went to bed and was looking forward to another day in a few hours.

Chapter Sixteen

Thanksgiving Dinner

In 18 years, this was the first time I would not have Thanksgiving Dinner with my family. Sergeant Downs had invited all the squad members to a Thanksgiving Dinner at his home. Thanksgiving morning with no wake-up call was a holiday for us; if we slept in, we'd miss breakfast. Some of us got up, ate breakfast, and then returned to bed for a few hours. Sergeant Downs lived about a mile from the front gate, and we could have taken a cab or walked. Dinner was going to start at 1300 hours. Getting back up and out of bed at about 1100 hours gave me ample time to get ready and head out to Sergeant Downs's home.

The front gate was less than half a mile from our barracks. All eight of us went to sign out in the orderly room and headed toward the front entrance. All we had to do at the front gate was to verify we had a pass to go off the base. A monument-like structure was just about across the street from the front entrance. The monument was the same structure that Hitler would stand on when visiting this military post as the German Leader. Hitler would give some of his speeches there. The main gate was also where hundreds of girls would stand by and wait to see if they could see Elvis, a famous singer/actor, when he was stationed here in Friedberg a few years earlier. It was a chilly Thanksgiving Day, so we took a cab to the house. Getting all eight of us to the sergeant's home took two cabs.

We arrived at our destination within a few minutes, and Sergeant Downs met us at the door. His wife was a wonderful person for making dinner for all of us. Their hospitality was very welcoming. Mrs. Downs directed us to the living room where her two children, a son, about 16 years old, and a daughter, who was 17, were. Sergeant Downs entered the living room, introduced his family, and informed us the dinner would be ready in about half an hour. We did arrive a little early because we took a cab instead of walking as planned earlier.

I was the youngest person in the squad, eighteen years old. Sergeant Downs's daughter took a liking to me. I wasn't interested in her because her father was my boss. I didn't need to get into trouble with him over his daughter. She did flirt with me; she would follow me every time I moved from room to room. Dinner was ready; we went into the dining room, and Mrs. Downs directed each of us where to sit. The two children stayed in the living room at a small coffee table where they would have dinner.

The Thanksgiving dinner was incredible, with turkey, gravy, potatoes, all the fixings, and good German beer. Sergeant Downs said grace with us, saying amen after his short Thanksgiving prayer. We all had a wonderful dinner, and it was home-like. After dinner, we all went to the living room to socialize and talk about the Thanksgiving we usually have at home. Sitting on the chair in the living room and enjoying an ice-cold beer, I could feel something tugging on my shirt. I turned around to look at what or who it might be. It was the Sergeant's daughter tugging on my shirt. Back then, just about every shirt had a small material loop on the back. It looks like a one-inch loop used to hang the shirt on a hook. The girl asked if she could rip it off my shirt as she had a collection of them. Sure, go ahead and rip it off. I've got more at the base in my closet. She ripped the one-inch loop right off my shirt. It surprised me that she would do it even if I gave her the okay; I thought she was teasing me, and she was.

After a while, Laton and Victor wanted to head to the Bahnhof bar. It wasn't too far to walk, still a little cool but not so cold that a nice walk wasn't bearable. We said our goodbyes, thanked the Downs family then left for the bar.

Walking down the small cobblestone streets, checking all the old and beautiful houses, noticing some of the buildings had what looked like slot machines attached to the side of the building. I walked up to one of the machines, and it was a German slot machine. It accepted ten pfennig coins. I played the device for a couple of minutes; needless to say, I lost about 1 DM. I also noticed that many homes had empty beer bottles by the doors. Layton told me why the empty beer bottles were hanging by the door. Here in Germany, they delivered door-to-door beer as the milkman delivered milk back home in the States.

Once we arrived at the Gasthaus, the bartender noticed us walking in. She pointed at Layton, asking him to come to see her as she wanted to talk with him. Layton and the bartender had a thing going, and we all knew it. We sat down as Layton neglected to acknowledge her call for him. After we sat, the bartender came over to the table for our order, which she already knew as we always ordered the same beer. We told her what we wanted to drink; the waitress went to the bar to get our drinks. When she returned with our beers, the waitress told Layton she had to talk to him out back. Layton excused himself from us at the table and left with her. Layton must have been with the bartender for about 10 minutes before returning to our table.

Victor asked Layton what critical matter she wanted to talk to him about. “Where the hell did you go”? Victor blurted out to Layton. His answer was he went up for a quickie. Victor and I looked at each other and wondered why Layton wanted sex with her. Layton explained he wasn’t in love but enjoyed having sex with her. Victor announced he was having his last beer and was returning to base. So, we got up and returned to base after finishing our beers. Walking a little over a mile was good for us, and it would sober us up a little before reaching the barracks.

The following morning, the wake-up call felt like it came up quickly. Sergeant Downs came into the squad room to give us a little heads-up. Sergeant Downs would receive information about the field maneuvers we would engage with. He told us we would be gone for about 14 days (two weeks). He would give us more details as time went on. Another thing coming up soon would be an EIB (Expert Infantrymen Badge) testing, which the drivers would be exempt from taking. Another benefit of being a driver is that some squad members thought I had an easy job.

Chapter Seventeen
European Infantry Badge, Testing

The company was getting ready for EIB testing, and as a driver, I was exempt from this testing. David was another driver in my platoon. He and I usually worked together while working in the motor pool on our tracks when I couldn't get Layton to help. I'm unsure where David was from; it was somewhere out west. When we had to change trackpads, we'd do it together. Once, we had to paint our tracks inside and outside; he and I helped each other on these projects. Another trooper, Robert, was also a track driver from the Company Office; he was from Skokie, Illinois. Robert and I were the same age and had much in common. Roberts was intimidated by some of the guys in our company.

After most of the day working on our tracks, we still had to communicate checks at the motor pool during the workday. The guys who went out for their EIB training were back for the day, so they also had to be present at the motor pool. After the communication checks, I locked up the track and returned to the company area with the rest.

After dinner, a few of us wanted to go to the Bahnhof Bar. It was either the Bahnhof Bar or the EM club. After cleaning up, we headed to the back gate; walking down to the bar didn't take long. Once at the bar, Layton returned to be with his girlfriend. The rest of us went to sit at a nearby Foosball table. That evening, we didn't play Foosball as the table was booked. “Beers for the table, please,” Victor shouted. The waitress served us within a few minutes. Soon, Layton showed up, and he wasn’t happy because his pregnant girlfriend wanted money from him to get an abortion. Laton was not the one to get her pregnant. If Layton were to part with his money, he’d buy more to drink. A girl across the room looked our way as we sipped our beer.

Layton ordered a round of beers for the table. I got up for a pee, a downfall of drinking beer. It seemed like every fifteen minutes, I had to pee. When arriving back at the table, sitting down, and taking another drink from my glass of beer, Layton looked at me and pointed toward the girl looking our way. He then asked me what I thought of the girl. She may have been about twenty-four years old. Layton and the guys knew I was a virgin and had never been with a girl for sex. I always enjoy being with girls, not for sex but for the friendly company. The girl finally headed to our table with her drink and asked if she could sit with us. Sitting next to me, Layton moved over and slid a chair between him and me; she then sat between us.

Her name was Mary; she spoke surprisingly good English. We talked with her and found out she worked on base at the P.X. snack bar. We often went for coffee at the snack bar but never paid much attention to who worked there. Mary asked me if I spoke German, and no was my answer. I told her I could speak some French and understood French better. Mary then asked me in French If I wanted to go to bed with her. In all my 18 years of living, Mary was the first person ever to ask me to bed. I turned her down, and all the guys at the table looked at me simultaneously. Not knowing the crew had set this up for me to lose my virginity that night. When we were ready to leave, the guys got up and looked at me, and said, " Have an enjoyable time." They would not let me go with them. Layton handed me a 50 Mark bill and left.

Mary told me she had a friend who operated a Gasthaus in the next town over in Nieder Wrolstad. We got up together then, and Mary grabbed my hand and drew me close to her as we left the Gasthaus. The Bahnhof was right across the street; once we arrived, we checked the schedules for the next train to Nieder Wrolstad. One would be leaving within ten minutes. I was nervous because I wasn't sure what to expect, unsure if I could satisfy her. While waiting for the train to arrive, we were making out on one of the benches on the platform.

The train arrived. We entered the train, Mary sat down, and I sat across from her. She got up and sat next to me and started kissing me again. I didn't mind that as I had kissing with many girls back home. Her tongue was deep into my mouth, and her actions aroused me. And she knew I was excited and moved her hands all over me. The train arrived at our stop; we got up and went to the exit doors to disembark the train. I never paid to have sex before because I never had sex. I asked Mary how much this would cost me, and she said she wasn't a whore and all I had to do was pay for the room. Once we entered the Gasthaus, her friend met us at the front desk. Mary's friend said it would be 5 DMs, which was about USD 1.25. As I mentioned, the dollar was worth much more than the DM. When I paid the girl, she gave me the brass key for the room on the second floor. I let Mary go first, thinking she would take me to the room, and I was right. I unlocked the door, and we entered the room. The room had a double bed, a chair, a small desk, and a sink with a small bathroom with a shower.

I sat on the bed, lit a cigarette, and then offered her one, which she accepted. So, I put another one to my lips and lit it for her. She sat next to me, and we talked a little to get to know each other better. When we finished smoking, she got up and started removing her clothes. Never seeing a naked girl was exciting to me. Mary had a great body and shape; her breasts were firm and perky, not too large. Still, with my clothes on, I moved up to her and caressed her beautiful breasts, we started to kiss each other, and she let me suck on her large nipples. She then began to take my clothes off. I had never done this before; it was another first for me. Having an idea there would be many first times going to happen to me that night.

Standing side by side naked as jaybirds, my manhood hard as a rock pulsating against her flat belly. Standing side by side nude with a girl had to be the best feeling I had ever felt. My brain thought I was going to hell because these views were not in God's will. Getting hotter and hotter, I guided Mary toward the shower and asked if she wanted to shower with me. She reached her hand into the shower stall and turned on the chilly water. We remained naked, kissing each other, and there wasn't enough room between us for anything. That's how close we were. We stepped inside, under the shower, the cold water dropping on our hot bodies, which I thought made me lose feelings somewhat. She grasped the bar of soap and began to wash my body from head to toe; now, Mary treated me. She soaped her hands and stroked me with her smooth hands. She then got on her knees and made me feel good, and I didn't want her to stop what she was doing. It didn't take long before it was over. It was the first time a woman sucked on my manhood and let it spit out in her face.

I wanted to soap her hot, beautiful, wet body as she did mine. Then, I took the soap bar, lathered it up, and rubbed it over her body. I never knew anything could feel this good. Her breasts were firm and beautiful compared to when Sandra pulled her sweater over my head; Sandra's breasts were huge, unbelievably soft, and felt soft compared to Mary's perky breasts. I soaped up and ran my hands all over her entire body. After this shower, we dried up and headed to bed for a wild night.

We went right into wild sex like a couple of animals. For some reason, Mary loved to be on top of me, and I didn't mind because this freed my hands so I could rub my hands all over Mary's body while having sex. We didn't sleep much that night. We did it several times that night: getting up early in the morning, going another round. When we left the bed, we dressed up and headed for another shower session. I told her I'd go to the PX snack bar to see her when I had the time, and she said OKAY.

Leaving the Gasthaus room, I left a 1 DM for a tip; Mary asked why I left a mark on the side table. I told her it was a tip. She took the one DM, put it in her pocket, and said that we do not tip in Germany; people get paid well. Before we left the Gasthaus, I stopped at the desk to call a cab to take her home and then back to Ray Barracks. I got back to base in time to make the first call.

After breakfast, we had a work call. The troops leaving for the EIB training had to get all their equipment and weapons. I didn't have time for the guys to ask me how it was last night. They had to get with the program; the rest of us drivers went down to the arms room as we would be cleaning the 50 caliber machine guns. The 50 caliber was the only weapon we could call a gun. Cleaning would take us till lunch. Around noon, I went to the PX snack bar. I saw Mary behind the counter, going to the lunch counter where she was. I said hi to her, and she said you don't talk to me when I'm working. After that day, I never saw her again.

I went back to the motor pool and got into the track, and with a ground guide, I drove the PC to the rear of the base, where I could show off and make doughnuts with the PC. I made a few doughnuts and then went to the wash rack to clean the track. After washing the PC, I went to the gas pumps and topped off. I arrived at the motor pool, and a ground guide would take me to my parking spot.

Not long after returning to the company, the guys out on the EIB training were arriving from the field. It was the last day the troops trained for EIB; the test would be in the morning. After the communication check, we returned to the barracks, and then Sergeant Downs went to the squad room. We had a brief discussion about the test. Sergeant Downs took me in the hallway and informed me that the platoon was short for troop testing. Sergeant Downs told me I must participate in the EIB testing in the morning. Holy shit was my first impression; I'm not ready for this crap. He told me I had no choice in the matter and that I'd better get some rest. There was no drinking tonight, so I got with the rest of the squad and took all the information I could for the test. Then Layton shouted across the room. He wanted to know how my date was. My face turned red, and then I called across the room, thanks, Layton, now I know what I've been missing.

Just then, this guy from the fourth squad came into our room. He was from Hawaii, and we called him Pineapple. He came in with a liter of whiskey and asked if we wanted a drink. I told him my twin had just received orders to Vietnam, and I needed a drink. That night, I drank till I passed out, face flat to the floor, another first for me. Thank you, US Army, for introducing me to consuming alcohol.

I woke up early the following day to prepare for EIB testing. Holy shit, I had the worst headache ever. After breakfast, we returned to the barracks to prepare for the test. Put on all our gear with our weapons and back into the formation. Some soldiers paired with someone who had previously completed the training process. This way, I would pass this exam. We went out to the FTA (Friedberg Training Area). We were trucked out there by two-and-a-half-ton trucks. Once we reached the training area, we were trained on what to expect and assigned them to groups of six. We had a starting point and a finishing point. We were given a map and a compass and informed that we had six hours to complete the test.

We headed out in small groups; we had to choose a leader to get us through the elements we would discover. I was selected to navigate with the map and compass and was good at map reading. We had to meet a timetable at particular locations. I was unaware there would be checkpoints as I didn't do any training after walking through the forest on our way to the first checkpoint. There were many obstacles to achieving from start to end. After reaching our first checkpoint, we headed to the next one. For this test, we had blanks for our rifles as we were to meet up with opposing teams. It was a sweltering day, and with all this gear on our backs, it wasn't easy. But it was a good thing we were young. After a few minutes, we were attacked by the opposing team.

We had one more checkpoint to go. The team was getting tired, and we would take a break. One of the team members took his poncho out of his bag, put it on the ground, and stretched it out flat. At this point, another trooper took out a pair of dice and wanted us to play crap while taking a break. They played, and I sat it out because I didn't understand the game and wasn't interested. About twenty minutes later, I tried to get the guys back on the road. It was getting dark, and we were behind on the test. One of the guys took the map out of my hands, ripped it up, and set it on fire. They were tired of listening to me as I gave directions so we could run and pass this test.

Without the map, we might say we were lost and had no idea where the last checkpoint was. We must have walked in circles for a while because I noticed a location we had just passed about half an hour earlier. We stopped for a break and tried to figure out the best way back out. After about thirty minutes, we came upon what we thought was the next checkpoint, but it wasn't. This checkpoint was the last, and we missed a checkpoint. Seeing it was getting late and we were the last team to complete the course, the scorekeepers told us we had finished, and passed the test. Then, we moved to where we had to board the trucks to reach the company area and stop for the day. We completed the course according to the paperwork. We passed, and that was the end of the EIB chapter.

Chapter Eighteen
Visit To The Dispensary

At about 0300 hours, I had to pee badly. I was only a few doors from the shower, and the bathroom was at the other end of the hallway. As I left my room, I could hear what sounded like a shower running from where I was. Sometimes, someone might go for a shower and forget to shut it off. I thought I'd see to ensure the water was off if nobody was there. Arriving in the doorway to the shower room, I could hear some moaning. Not thinking, I rushed in to ensure nobody fell on the shower floor. To my surprise, someone was in the shower. I didn't want to see what I saw. It was someone from my platoon, but of another squad, that's right, the moaning I heard was someone relieving himself in the shower. I tried to be quiet; I turned around and headed to the hallway lavatory at the other end.

Son of a bitch, when I started to pee, I could feel a little discomfort in my penis. I thought to myself, I've seen enough movies about VD. I knew what I got from that one-night stand. I guess I had nobody to blame but myself. With this inside my head, my thoughts were, what am I to do? Knowing the only thing to do was go to the dispensary in the morning. Not that easy; if I went to see the doctors, how would the guys feel about me not taking precautions when having sex? I waited for a few days to get enough nerve to face reality and headed to the doctor. The longer I waited, the more pain I had when I urinated.

During the morning work call, I told Sergeant Downs my problem and that I needed to go to the dispensary after breakfast. After work call formation, I headed out to take care of things. I wasn't the only person to visit the dispensary; I had to wait in line to be seen by a doctor. One of the doctors called my name, and I went into the doctor's office to face the music. The doctor asked me about my symptoms. After telling him, he told me to take my shirt off and gave me a shot of penicillin. He then told me to return if things were not any better in a couple of days. As I put my shirt back on, the doctor told me I could return to work and not forget to wash my hands often.

After leaving the doctor's office, I headed to the motor pool, knowing some team members would be there. Sergeant Downs gave me back the keys to the track, and he then left, leaving me alone. Just before leaving, he told me to wash the track. An hour and a half later, I took a break and headed to the PX coffee shop to see if Mary was there. Once at the coffee shop, I went to the counter and asked if Mary was there. I learned Mary no longer worked for the Coffee shop.

I left the coffee shop a little disappointed Mary wasn't working there anymore because I wanted to thank her for the damn clap; I was upset at that bitch. I guess I'll never see the girl who took my virginity away in vain. So that's it, a whore took my virginity, and I will never know anything about her. I could also have gotten her pregnant, and I'll never know; hoping she was on the pill. Oh well, then, I went back to the motor pool to get the track washed. At the wash racks, while cleaning the track, I started to get a bit lightheaded. I started developing other systems due to the penicillin shot I had just received. I noticed that my face was getting numb. I passed my hand over my face, and I could not feel my hand on my face. Next, I was starting to get a reaction and feeling worse. I left the track at the wash racks and locked it up. I hurried to the dispensary to tell someone I had a penicillin shot a few hours earlier and started with my systems. No sooner had I told the doctor what was happening. He ripped off my shirt and yelled to an aid that I could have penicillin reactions. After my shirt was off, the doctor and his aide shoved needles into my arms. I had four shots; I was taken to a room with a bed, instructed to lie down, and that they would investigate me in a few minutes.

During my short stay at the dispensary, my temperature shot up to 103 degrees. I was sweating and felt cold enough to call for someone into the room and ask them to get me a few blankets because I was freezing. Finally, I fell asleep and got the rest that I desperately needed. I woke up several times because of the itching and fever and fell asleep.

While asleep, I had one of the most beautiful dreams/visions ever. I dreamed of walking on a beach on the most beautiful white sand. The sand felt like silk under my bare feet. The sun was bright, the smooth, warm breeze rounding around my naked body. Just walking along the beach, I noticed that there was not one soul around. It was so quiet that I thought I had entered heaven. After a few minutes of walking, I saw what looked like a white Dove gliding my way. As I walked toward the Dove, it seemed like it was flying away from me. I heard a voice that I thought was of an angel. I turned around to see where the voice was coming from but still didn't see anybody. I kept walking on this peaceful beach and heard a voice call from a distance.

At a far distance, I could see a figure like an angel; by this time, I knew I had to have been in heaven—a form shaped like a woman was getting closer. The young woman had a sheer see-through robe on her body. I heard her voice calling, but she wasn't calling me by name. The closer I got to the young woman, the better I could listen to her calling me. By now, we were standing face to face on this beautiful beach, not one other person besides us. I reached out my hand to this angel-like woman, and she reached to me, but we could not touch each other for some reason. I asked her what her name was, and she answered; she said it to me in the softest-spoken voice. You may call me Love, and at this time, our hands touched. Looking at her body, I saw she was perfect; therefore, I knew an angel had visited me.

With the sun shining on both of us, I could see that Love had a perfect body that only an angel could have. She had the most perfectly shaped body of an angel. After our hands met, the weather started to change. The wind was picking up, getting cloudy, and the weather turned. Still holding hands with Love, the wind was picking her off the beach, and I didn't want to let her go. The angel Love spoke a few more words to me. I will save a place for you when it's your time. The wind pulled Love away, with my hands reaching out toward her. She moved with the wind, leaving me to go toward the heavens.

Waking up again, I felt better; I called for someone who might have been a nurse or an aid and asked if I could return to my unit. She took my stats and said I seemed to be doing well. All I had to do was sign out of the dispensary, and I could be on my way. I felt hungry after leaving the bed and dressed up when I saw it was time for a communication check at the motor pool. I thought I'd better head toward the company area for the last formation of the day. Most people in the company formation were looking at me, and I could not figure out why the soldiers were all looking at me.

Before being dismissed to the motor pool, the company commander addressed me and said he wanted to see me in the orderly room ASAP. I went to the office as ordered and waited to see the captain. The captain opened the office door and asked why I had been AWOL for the last three days. My reaction was, what do you mean? I've never missed a company formation since I've been with the company. He asked me what day it was, and I responded it was Tuesday. He looked puzzled and said it was Friday and I had been missing for three days. I told him I had gone to the dispensary for a drug reaction but couldn't have been there for more than a few hours. The captain called the dispensary for verification; he told me my answer was correct and that I should take the rest of the day off and get some rest. Then, he asked to see me tomorrow and off I went.

I lost three days of my life and didn't realize it until afterward. Another first for me, and now finding out I had an allergy to penicillin. Not long after I lay on my bed, the guys came into the room to see what had happened to me. The guys felt terrible for setting me up with a woman who had VD. I told the squad not to worry and that I had recovered from the penicillin shot and cured of the clap.

Sergeant Downs came into the room and asked if there was anything he could do for me. I thanked him for his concerns and told him I was healthy. After Sergeant Downs left the squad room, the guys came around me and asked what had happened to me and why I had gone for three days. I told them I had contacted the clap from the only girl I had ever had sex with in my entire life. I also asked the guys to please not set me up with any other girls as this scared me about sex.

Layton told me there was live entertainment at the EM club and asked if I wanted to go with them. He told me the guys were going to the club early as the place would get packed that night. The guys were all going to the club for dinner instead of the mess hall. I'd love to go to the club for dinner and the show; Layton told me we would meet at 1800 hours.

I found out the live music playing at the club that night was from a famous women's singing group from the States. I do not remember her name. After cleaning up and taking a hot shower, I dressed casually for the night out. I arrived at the club just a little before 1800 hours, and the club was jam-packed with people. When a particularly famous guest group played at the club, some locals would come to the club if military personnel escorted them. We could have a satisfying dinner at the club for $2.50, a pretty good deal.

After the show, I returned to the barracks alone; the walk took only a few minutes. I was not to walk alone after dark; back in the '60s, the racial riots also affected the military bases across Germany. Some nights, there would be racial fighting break out on base and sometimes in some of the clubs in downtown Friedberg.

I went back, entered my room without an incident and discovered that my wall locker had been broken into. I always kept a can of change in my wall locker, a habit I followed since high school. I wanted to find out who did this to me. I would find a way to protect my can of change.

At the mail call, I received a letter from my twin brother telling me he requested a 1049 transfer to Friedberg, Germany. We were simultaneously three brothers in the US Army, which must have significantly stressed our mother. In his letter, Gil said his commander honed his request because he had done a fantastic job working for him. After his present court case job was over, he'd be on his way to Germany. Gil told me he should arrive in Germany in about two months. I was happy to hear this great news.

The following day, I went to the motor pool to seek help to booby-trap my wall locker. One of the mechanics gave me a great idea of how to booby-trap my locker. He gave me a recharged used Jeep battery. I could wire the two handles on my wall locker to the battery, so if anybody tried to break into it, they would get a minor non-fatal jolt.

Specialist Stevens was our company clerk, and he was also the person who would deliver our mail during mail calls at the last daily formation. Stevens and I got to be friends, and one day, he asked if I wanted to go out nightclubbing with him some night. Saturday would be okay with me. After a mail call, we made plans for Saturday, and he had been stationed in Friedberg about six months before I arrived. I wasn't sure about this guy, but we were in the same company.

Stevens said there was a bar in Bad Nauheim; it was just the next town over. We took a cab to the club. It was like an underground club, with a cover charge that wasn't too expensive. It cost two Marks to enter, and once inside, we found a place to sit. It wasn't long before two girls asked to sit with us, and Stevens invited them to sit. These girls were hookers looking to make money from us and make some money for the bar owner. When a girl sat down, they asked us to buy them a drink. When they ordered their drinks, they asked for a whiskey and coke on the side. These girls could drink all night long without getting drunk. Once they started to drink, they'd get friendly, play with us, and get us aroused. We'd buy them more drinks in hopes they would get intoxicated, and then we might find pleasure with them. Here was their secret: they drank the whiskey, quickly placed the glass of coke on their lips, and spit it into the glass. We only bought two drinks for the girls, and when we refused to purchase them another drink, they got up and left for another table. That's when we noticed the Coke glasses had more volume; this is when we figured out what they were doing.

Later in the evening, a strip show was in the next room. The bartender of the event would announce it fifteen minutes before the show. We'd have to leave the room and go to another room. We were not allowed to bring our drinks but had to order a new drink across the hall in the other room. We went without the girls, and the room was full of people who wanted to see the show. Someone locked the door to the room where the strip show was going.

As we sat down, a waitress asked what we wanted to drink. We ordered, and not long after, four girls came out. The music started playing, and their clothing came off when they were gesturing to do so. These girls were OK and great looking, even better than the little slut Mary that gave me the clap. I focused on the girls; this was the second time I had seen a girl without clothes. These girls had rigid bodies. They had nice-sized, perky breasts and danced utterly naked, not a stitch of clothing on their bodies. A show like this indeed turned the guys on.

The show took approximately fifteen minutes, and we had to leave the room shortly afterward. We returned to the room where we were at first and had to order more drinks. What a racket; they knew how to make money from us military boys.

We left after we had finished our drinks. We went outside; cabs lined up, waiting to taxi the troops back to base. We always had the cab driver take us to the back gate next to our barracks. After 2200 hours and feeling pretty good, I went to bed for a well-deserved rest.

Chapter Nineteen

Preparing For a Two-Week Field Maneuvers

This morning, after company formation, Sergeant Downs assembled us in the squad room to inform us about the field maneuvers. We were about to go out again soon, this time for two weeks. Graff would be where we would be going for more training. This area was near the Czechoslovakian border, about 340 km from Friedberg. It would take overnight to get there by train because train transportation for the military was always getting the last priority on the tracks. We will be getting ready for this trip in the next few days.

As a track driver, I would spend much time ensuring the vehicle was combat-ready for our planned trip to Grafenwöhr. While the rest of the team went to classes to prepare for this training, we drivers went to the motor pool to do a complete checklist on the tracks. If I couldn't do the work on the track, I would have to get help from the maintenance department. We drivers always worked together when it came to the tracks. On this day, Sergeant Downs would be with me, working and preparing for this mission. It was essential for us to have these training programs as plenty of money was being spent on them to show strength to the Soviet Union and East Germany.

After breakfast, we made the work formation. The driver and squad leaders headed to the motor pool while the remaining troops went to classrooms for the rest of the day. We stopped at a small coffee shop on our way to the motor pool. Sergeant Downs was a kind person; he paid for the coffee, which was ten cents each. When we arrived at the track, I opened the track and started up the engine to lower the rear ramp. I opened the hood to the engine compartment to check all the oils and filters. Sergeant Downs had a checklist to go by. We started at the top of the list and went through it all. I did have to get a few trackpads replaced. It wasn't a tough job. Sergeant Downs went home for lunch, and I headed to the mess hall for lunch.

After lunch, the guys and I went to the squad room to wait for the afternoon formation, and from there, I went back to the motor pool to finish the work on the track. Sergeant Downs didn't come with me as he had to teach one of the classes in the afternoon. All I had left was to replace a few trackpads; I had help from another track driver. When we finished replacing the pads, I drove my truck to the wash racks to wash the vehicle's exterior and then to the fuel depot to top it off with gas. Then, the track was combat-ready.

I wanted to go to Frankfurt for the evening, and I had to find someone to accompany me. While in the orderly room signing for a pass, I checked out who had also signed out for Frankfurt, spotting Stew's name. I went to see him and asked if I could join him in Frankfurt. He and two others who were going to Frankfurt didn't mind. We never go to Frankfurt alone to nightclubbing. We had to do the buddy system. At this point, four of us were going to the city. I enjoyed going with Layton and Victor, but they only wanted to go to the EM club or the Bahnhof Bar in Friedberg.

When ready, we walked to the train station and waited for the train. Traveling on the train was almost daily for us soldiers; it wasn't too expensive, maybe four to five Marks round trip, and we'd be in Frankfurt in about 25 minutes. Frankfurt has many pubs and clubs near the Bahnhof; one of our favorite bars was the Myergouster. This bar served tasty food and good beer. Once in the club, we looked for a table to accommodate the four of us. Telephones connected to the table lamps were on the tables, and a number on each lampshade matched the phone number. If you see someone in the club you'd like to dance with, you must call that table and ask to meet on the dance floor. We had no idea who was calling for a dance until they came to the dance floor and met the caller.

The bathroom was on the lower level, and I had to pee badly. If you had the money on the way to the bathroom, there were a few games to play. I went into the bathroom, and there was a male attendant dressed like a butler. He was standing next to a small table holding some hand wipes, toilet paper, condoms, a small bottle of water, hand pump soap, and a small dish on the table with a few coins in it. I went to the urinal, which was the wall; that's right, we peed on the walls: the tin-covered walls and a trough guided the urine to the drain near the floor. Before exiting the bathroom, I had to pass in front of this butler. I washed my hands and went over to the table to get my hands dried. I lifted my hands before the butler, and he took a wipe off the table and dried my hands for me. Now I know I had to leave him a tip, and I dropped a fifty-pfennig piece as a tip. That was another first for me: someone watching me pee and washing my hands.

Outside of the bathroom was what looked like an arcade. There was a shooting gallery that I just had to play. I put a coin into the machine and started shooting the targets. A lady kept talking to me, which was irritating, so I asked her what she wanted. She wanted me to go back upstairs and buy her a drink. I told her not to bother me as I was trying to play a game. She was a pretty-looking girl, maybe in her early thirties. An older lady stood not far from me and heard me tell the other girl not to bother me. This other lady must have been in her late forties; she grabbed me by the arm and asked if I would buy her a drink. My answer was no, but the younger girl stuck between us and insisted I buy her a drink. The two girls started yelling and pushing each other over who I would buy a drink. It was the first time I'd ever had two girls fight for me, another first for me.

I left and went back upstairs to be with the guys. A few minutes after sitting down and taking another sip of my beer, the phone on the table rang. I answered it, and someone wanted me to go to the dance floor for a dance with me as I was the one to answer the call. I got up and went to the dance floor, just as I thought it was one of those girls I saw down by the arcade. She certainly was a beautiful lady with blond hair and stunning blue eyes. Her name was Petra, and we danced slowly on the dance floor. And she held me tight, and I was doing the same. I knew there was no air between our bodies; dancing a slow dance as we did was complex, but I enjoyed it big time.

I wanted to buy her a drink; as we sat down, the server came to the table to see if we wanted to order more. Petra ordered a drink. I watched her take the whiskey and take a sip, and then take the glass of coke, and I could tell she spit the whiskey in the glass that held the coke. Petra rubbed her hand on me and whispered in my ear that she wanted another drink. I turned and looked at her and planted my lips on hers. Our tongues mingled for a few seconds as all the guys at the table looked at us. I told her I'd buy her another drink after she finished drinking the rest of the Coke. Petra said she had to pee; she left to not be seen again that night. It was getting late; we had to catch the train back to Friedberg. The Bahnhof was just a few minutes from this nightclub; off we went back to Friedberg.

We walked to the back gate right behind our barracks when we arrived at Friedberg. After entering the barracks, I entered the orderly room to sign in. The company clerk on duty handed me a note from the Company Commander. The message said my twin was at the 3rd Armored Division in Frankfurt, and I should call him in the morning. Hearing this was exciting news for me, and I'm sure my brother was excited, too.

When I returned to the room, I told the guys about my twin brother being in Frankfurt, wishing I had known this earlier in the day. I could have seen him while I was in Frankfurt; I'll get to talk to him in the morning. I'll request a day off from Sergeant Downs to visit my brother in Frankfurt. I have never asked for a personal day off before, but I know some of the guys who lived off post have asked for personal days out and would get it.

The next day, I saw Sergeant Downs after the first call, and told him that my brother was in Frankfurt at Division Headquarters. He already knew Gil was coming to Germany. He said he'd get back to me and had to run it through with the Company Commander. After the work formation, Sergeant Downs told me it was acceptable to take the day off to see my brother. Right then, I went to the orderly room to sign out on a day pass. I quickly went to my room, changed into my street clothes, and headed for the Bahnhof. Sergeant Downs offered to drive me to the station. On our way to the station, he wanted to talk to me about re-enlisting in the Army. I told him I'd been in the Army for only a year and a half. That didn't matter, he said to me, and there was a re-enlistment bonus of four thousand dollars. Arriving at the station while exiting his car, I told him I'd consider it.

I arrived in Frankfurt and took a cab from the Bahnhof to the 3rd Armored Division on Hamburger Landstrass, not knowing there was a train substation just a few hundred meters away from where Gil was staying. Upon arriving at Drake Edward Kaserne, I asked the security guard at the front gate how to reach the building where my brother worked. He checked my papers and ID card, called for him, and he came to the gate. We had much to catch up on, so we went to the Post Exchange snack bar for lunch.

I asked Gil why he didn't come to Friedberg as his orders read. He told me he had been in Frankfort for three days. His MOS (Military Occupational Specialty) worked as an office clerk. After comparing notes from the last year when we hadn't seen each other, he took me to his living quarters. Compared to mine, Gil had a wonderful place in a two-person room. I told Gil I was going on field maneuvers in a few days. When I returned, I'd come over for a visit and show him around the City of Frankfurt. Gil later took me to his place of work to meet his co-workers. His boss was a Full Bird Colonel heading up the division supply. His boss told Gil he could take a couple of hours off so he and I could have an Open Mess lunch. Instead of the open mess hall, we went to the EM club for lunch. There was a more extensive menu there. After lunch, Gil and I returned to his office, where he introduced me to the people he worked with. Gil would be known as Roy-One, and I would be as Roy-Two.

Chapter Twenty
Grafenwöhr
Two Weeks Field Maneuvers

The morning of the field trip to the Grafenwöhr training area was upon us. The night before, most troops went to the Post Exchange to pick up personal supplies like snacks, soda, cigarettes, and other items we could not purchase in the field, or so I believed. Some vending trucks were allowed in the training area, but we didn't know if we'd had time to visit those trucks.

The railhead was just behind our base, where we would go to mount our vehicles on the flatbed rails cars. We headed to the motor pool after the work call. I was the track driver, and my job was to pick someone to the arms room to pick up the M50 caliber machine gun. Once at the motor pool, I unlocked the track and dropped the ramp to place the machine gun in the track. My job was to ensure I had all the tie-down equipment needed to secure the track on the flatbed. We were going down the checklist.

Sergeant Downs was with me if I needed some aid. The railhead was about a mile from the base, so we had to walk or march back. Mounting all our Brigades' vehicles on the flatbed cars was difficult. These cars would sometimes stretch out a long way. The first vehicles to mount the flatbed cars had to drive from the first flatbed car to the end, which might have been thirty flatbed cars. There would be trucks, jeeps, tanks, howitzers, other tracked vehicles, and anything with wheels that would be necessary on this trip. It came to my turn to drive my track on board.

Sergeant Downs was my guide, and He was my eyes as I could not see the positions of my tracks on the flatbed. My tracks were overhanging the flatbed car by two inches on both sides. It was a slow and delicate movement; as this was my first time doing this, I had to drive on about fourteen flatbed cars. Once we were in a position on the site, we could start to tie down.

Sergeant Downs and I started with putting trigs in front of the track, identical to the rear of the track. After we had that done, we continued with the tie-down equipment. Fastening Steel cables and clamps had to be done by hand; thus, we had to wear gloves to avoid getting cut by these rough steel cables. It took more than three hours from start to finish to complete this task.

After all the vehicles were on the train flatbeds, we headed back to the barracks with one stop on the way. There was a small Gasthaus not far from the railhead, and we made a quick stop for a coffee and a relaxing walk back to the barracks. Once I returned to the squad room, I packed my belongings into my duffel bag. We also had to strip out our beds and secure and lock all our belongings. We had about an hour before the two-and-a-half-ton trucks would arrive to pick us up. The trucks were to transport us from the company; being Charlie Company, we'd be the third group shipped from our battalion.

The company commander went through each room to ensure that everyone was present and accounted for and that nobody was drunk. Going on the maneuver meant we would have some nights that we would not have any of that good German Beer. After the commander had finished, he told us to board the trucks.

Once off the trucks, we walked through the railroad yard, careful not to trip or fall as we hauled our equipment. It was dark out, so we had to use our flashlights to see where we were walking to avoid tripping over the rails. As I was walking, I heard a few pops. I stopped as others did to what the sounds of broken bottles were. It happened to be some bottles of soda pop someone had stuffed inside their jacket that had fallen from his coat as they were not very well secured. They broke as they hit the ground.

We walked across tracks and between boxcars and finally arrived at our allocated car. We all had compartments where half a dozen soldiers slept. After settling in, we felt the train start to move. We then tried to get some sleep. We'd be in these compartments overnight. There were bathrooms at each end of the car marked WC. The train hurried when it was not in some train yard. We could look out the windows and see the rest of the train behind us with all those vehicles following us. We fell asleep, and when we woke, it was daylight, and breakfast was ready. Not much of a breakfast, we were each given a box of C-rations. These C-rations were designed to serve the World War II military. That is correct; these rations were over 20 years old. Some of these rations gave some of us the runs, which was not too funny. The train didn't move out during the busy time of the day. Some of the guys would take a walk to see how many cars they could walk through without being stopped.

I had a deck of cards that lightened the guys in the compartment. I had a double deck of pinochle cards that took four people to play. We had just the correct number of people to play with; this kept us busy for a while, and it did pass the time. Occasionally, someone would want to sit in and play some cards, but no one would give up their seat.

The day went by, and the train started to move again. Each meal on this trip was C-rations, not the best of foods, and I remembered what the recruiter told me: three hot meals and a bed—no hot meals that day. I was lied to again, but there was not much I could do about that.

We just got word that we should reach our destination within two hours, and Sergeant Downs told us to be prepared and ready when the train stopped. All the drivers were to get off the train first so we could go to our vehicles to get ready to drive off the rail cars. Sergeant Downs and I got together to see how we would handle this part of the trip. We went to the dining car for a meeting. All drivers and track commanders were there to receive instructions for our next move. By the time the meeting with all instructions was over. The train approached the stop and didn't stop at the station but at the train yard railhead.

We got off the train and headed toward the flatbed cars. I unlocked the driver's hatch and then opened the center hatch to get some tools out. Sergeant Downs and I went right over to take down the tie-down equipment, placed it on the top of the track, and secured it safely. I was ready to drive the track off the flatbeds but had to wait our turn. There were many vehicles ahead of my track. It was close to an hour before we got off the rail cars. The other soldiers were waiting for us at a nearby parking lot.

I pulled into the parking lot with the rest of the company track drivers, seventeen tracks in our company, one jeep for the company commander, and the mess truck. We drove in convoy toward the Grafenwöhr training area. After arriving, we had to set up tents where we would make our home for the next two weeks. These tents were large enough to accommodate our platoon's four squads.

Once our platoon was all present, we formed around the platoon leader, Sergeant Bundy. He gave us instructions on how to pitch this tent. The first thing was to lay out the tent across the concrete pad. Then, we had to place the short tent poles on the outside of the tent, insert the poles into the holes in the tent, and raise the poles upwards. Once all the short poles were in place, three people grabbed one of the longer poles and went under the canvas to place the pole in the center hole. After the tent was up, we had to set up two coal-burning stoves as it got cold in the evening. We had cots and a sleeping bag. The recruiter mentioned cots to me, three meals, and a cot. I guess I couldn't complain about that one.

It took the rest of the day to get our things together. The place looked pretty good for being in a tent. The motor pool wasn't too far from the tent. The commander called for company formation, and we all went out as directed. The company commander took a roll call, and all were in attendance. We were informed what to expect for the next few days. Then, we were dismissed for dinner and headed to the mess tent. This place resembles the TV show 4077 Mash, living in tents and eating out of steel trays.

Still not dark yet, I walked around the motor pool. I'm glad I did because I saw A friend named Tom from home. I didn't know he was in the Army. We had a lot to catch up on about each other. There was a smaller tent not far from my tent, and it was a beer tent. We were allowed to have a couple of beers before bedtime. Tom and I did that, had a few beers, and discussed old times and our future. We had our last sip of beer, left, and never met again while in the Army.

We returned to the tent, which looked larger inside than outside. The inside of the tent was not as neat as our barracks back in Friedberg. We were not allowed to take the beer out of the beer tent. It was tough to resist not taking beer from the beer tent. About half of the troops in my tent took a beer from the beer tent; all we had to do was slide the beer under our jackets. Sergeant Downs walked into the tent and caught us drinking some beer. We had to dump the rest of what we had, and he told us he'd let this slide by, but not a second time. Sergeant Downs didn't want to look bad if this had been reported to the Company Commander, as it would go into the books. So, we were lucky he didn't report us and give us a personal warning.

The next morning was Sunday, a day off for us, so the next training didn't start until Monday morning. We got out of bed at about 0700 hours, cleaned up, and used the facilities to go out of the tent to the bathhouse. The facilities were not very sanitary toilets, but we were simulating a war situation and had to do what we had.

Having left our tent and going to the mess tent for breakfast, we had to dress up warmly; it was cold. While sitting at breakfast, Sergeant Hallee came over to me and asked if I was a Catholic, and my response to him was yes. That was a mistake because he wanted me to attend a Sunday morning service. Sergeant Hallee outranked me, and I was only a specialist four, so I told him I would go. Sergeant Hallee informed me that the church service started in half an hour, and he wanted to see me there. I wouldn't say I liked attending church service today, listening to the same old sermons. One time, when I attended Catholic School, the Church read the whole Bible every three years, so being 18 years old, I must have heard the priest read the bible about six times and never got anything out of it. Thus, during the remainder of my time in the Army, after attending church service that day, I didn't participate in any more church services.

After Church service, I spoke with Sergeant Hallee and informed him that I didn't want to attend any more church services. He wasn't happy that I didn't want anything to do with the Catholic Church. Still, he did understand going to a church to satisfy someone besides God would make me a Hippocratic.

Sergeant Downs called for me, and I saw him at the NCO's tent. We talked about the condition of the track, and he wanted to go to the motor pool and check out the track with me to be sure it was up to speck.

Once at the motor pool, I unlocked my track. I started the track and then dropped the back ramp. We checked to see if all our C-rations were on board and all the ammo was on board. I'd hate to find out what would happen to me if any of the C-rations or ammo was missing. All was in order and ready to go for the morning training. I also took a few minutes to make sure the heater in the track was in working condition, which it was. At this time of the year, we need a good running heater.

I returned to the tent and wrote a few letters home to some friends. When I first joined the Army, I wrote letters all the time, but as time passed, I wrote less and less. I did keep on writing to Gail from Bolton, England. Gail was the biggest reason I signed up for four years. Enlisting for four years gave me the guarantee of being stationed in Europe. I will take the following leave to go to England to visit Gail and her family. Bonnie, a friend back home, had stopped writing to me. She must have made friends with another boy, but he did not want her to write to me. Ellen, the daughter of a Maine Senator for the State of Maine, also had stopped writing.

Layton and King were heading to the beer tent and asking if I wanted to join them. It did not take much persuading to put my letter writing away, and out of the tent, I went with the boys. I set myself to two beers a night while out on training. Damn, I saw someone on the other end of the beer tent who looked like someone who lived next door to me in civilian life. I went over to talk to the person, and it was my old neighbor, Paul, my brother Jeff's classmate. We spoke briefly; I was in the Army before Paul's draft. Paul was in the same division I was in but was stationed in Bad Homburg, ten miles from Friedberg. After a few minutes, I sat with my team members. I told my team I had met a friend from my hometown.

After the second beer, I left the tent and headed to the lavatory before entering the platoon tent for the night. There would be a different person for the guard duty at each tent, and drivers were exempt.

The first thing the following day after breakfast, we all marched to the motor pool and mounted onto the tracks. As the track driver, this would be my first time going on tank trails. Tank trails were like tote roads, with no pavement, just dirt, dust, and sometimes water and mud. Most tank trails were like roller coasters, with hills and dips. I had control of the track and could see where I was going, but the troops inside could not see anything. It was like they were in a box with no windows; I'm sure they bounced around a lot.

I drove toward the forest and did training on how to attack the enemy. All our team vehicles had red bands, and the opposing team had blue bans on their vehicles. The war games were exciting, and this sure was realistic. If the blue team hit my track, I'd be out of the game. We were lucky because we were in the game till the end. I'd drive up to the target and drop the ramp, then the troops and the squad leader would exit the track. Then, I raised the ramp and backed away to hide because I did not want to be hit by enemy fire.

After a while, the war game was interrupted for lunch; I drove the track to where the troops were. We were to go to the company mess truck for food. We circled the mess truck like in the olden days as the wagons made a circle when attacked; we all know how that ended.

After lunch, we headed for our next training area, which would be at the range to fire the 50-caliber machine gun. The teams fired machine guns while I was driving the track. It was something else, and I could feel the track jerk at each round fired. After each team member had taken turns firing the 50 caliber, I was obliged to stop the track, and the Track Commander and I swapped places. Sergeant Downs got behind the laterals, and I mounted up behind the 50 Caliber to take my turn at firing the machine gun. Firing the 50 caliber wasn't like firing a rifle. I got to feel the power of that machine gun, and it was a wonderful experience.

After the 50 caliber firing range, we retreated from training for the day and returned to base camp. I had to clean the track and replenish supplies at the camp motor pool. Sometimes, we may have had to use some of the ammo we had on the track. I took the track to the wash rack for cleaning; one of the guys had to help me, and it was Victor. Victor was an immense help to me; he was like a mentor but not as good as Layton. On returning to the motor pool, I stopped to top off the track with gas and checked my oils and trackpads.

Back at the platoon tent, we were all gathered inside the tent and given the critique for the day's operations. We critiqued how we did as a company team and how the platoon did as a team. Every time we were not using our weapons, we had to keep them locked up in the Arms Truck, and that was Earnest's job as he was the arms room clerk. After I had cleaned around my bunk and straightened up, I headed out to the mess tent for another excellent meal. Sitting with Layton and Victor, we enjoyed the meal the excellent cooks had prepared. They did very well in getting our meals. Back at the tent, I took a little time to catch up on my mail and newspapers. After going through the newspapers, I had no problem because someone always wanted to read the news from home.

We did not get much communication with the outside world while in the field. No TV sets and not many had radios with them. As usual, I had a letter from my mother and also from Gail of Bolton, England. Gail asked if I knew when I'd come over to England for a visit we'd been talking about for over a year. In reply, I told her I would apply for two weeks' leave to take that long-awaited trip. I answered my mother's letter and let her know Gil and I had already met. We would get together once I returned from the field to Ray Barracks.

Some guys went to the beer tent, and I asked whether I could join them. The day's highlight was being out in the field, drinking, and getting drunk. The Army recruiter back home, Sergeant Kirk, didn't tell me that I would become an alcoholic in a brief time. It seemed like I was drinking daily and nightly. What else was I to do? I had worked myself up to an E-4 Specialist and was soon looking to be an E-5. Let's go before we lose the good seats. That was a joke, as all seats in the beer tent were good, with tables and chairs and a makeshift bar at the other end of the tent. A bunch of pallets stacked on each other with a sheet of plywood made it look like a table.

Sergeant Downs entered the beer tent, sat with us, and discussed what we'd do the next day. The next day, we would not be going out for training as I would have to work on the track with Sergeant Downs, getting the track ready for a pass and review in front of a grandstand with many people watching us pass by. This pass and review would include all the troops from our Brigade and all the vehicles.

The next day, Sergeant Downs and I went to the motor pool to work on the track; we had to replace two other trackpads. Everything else was looking perfect. Whenever I had a moment, I'd love to work on the track; it was my pride and joy.

The morning of the pass and review has arrived. This pass and review were supposed to show our admiration for the world, with Czechoslovakia just a few miles away from where we were, East Germany not far away, or, of course, the USSR. After the pass and review and the other planned events, we were to get ready to return to Friedberg the following day.

The pass and review started, and we were in line and waiting on two hills that held us all in order. There was lots of planning for this parade. There was no pedestrian traffic at this parade; all military vehicles drove three abreast at about 15 miles per hour. It took about a half hour for this whole Brigade to pass the reviewing stand. Once the pass and review were over, an air and ground show showed our military's mighty firepower. Jets came flying over the grandstand, flew a couple of miles, and fired upon the target, all kinds of explosions from the rockets and bombs falling on the target. After the air strikes, the ground force showed their power with all types of firepower. This display was outstanding and spectacular; someone had to be there to see for themselves.

Sergeant Downs said we would begin packing in the morning due to the completed mission. I could not wait to return to Friedberg to visit my brother in Frankfurt. After the short meeting with Sergeant Downs and all the instructions we were to follow the next day to prepare for our return, we headed out to the mess tent for our night meal. After we had eaten dinner, Sergeant Downs invited the squad members to the beer tent, and he'd spring for the first rounds of beers to show appreciation for a job well done.

Even out in the field, we could get good beer. Heineken was my favorite beer, but it was a little more expensive than the beer from the local brewery. We each had a couple of beers and returned to the tent to prepare for the move back to home base. We weren't leaving the following day but just getting ready; being in the field for a couple of weeks seemed like a long time, so we were excited about returning to the post and back to normal.

I packed things into my duffel bag and only kept out clothing that I would wear for the trip back to Ray Barracks. On the trip back, I would allow the guys to put their bags in the track even though we were not allowed to. I did check with Sergeant Downs before giving the guys the okay. Layton snuck in a few beers, and enough for the team. We cleaned the outside of the tent and inside it as well as possible to make it easy for us when it came down.

Reveille again was quickly upon us. Today would be a hectic day for us all. There is much work and planning to make a massive move like this. Moving 2,000 troops and many vehicles back to the Friedberg area, I'm sure a move like this was costly. We all attended the morning company meeting to get orders on what would take place for the next few days. We played an essential role in this massive move back to home base.

After breakfast, all squad leaders met with their squad to discuss the big move. This move would be more complex than our move to arrive here at the Grafenwöhr training area. Sergeant Downs assigned

Layton to work with me as he noticed Layton was deeply knowledgeable. We packed all we could in our duffel bags and set them aside to transfer them to the track. We did an excellent job cleaning the inside tent and the outside of the tent.

Sergeant Downs and I headed to the motor pool. Sergeant Downs wouldn't stay with us. Instead, he stayed with us long enough to ensure we did the job correctly. After the Sergeant's departure, the platoon Sergeant was in charge. I had to drive the track to the railhead and then move the track on the flatbed rail cars. It was a long wait as the vehicles loaded onto the flatbeds; the wheeled vehicles went on first, then the tracked vehicles followed. My turn came up, and I was ready for the rail flatbeds to drive on. I was careful not to drive off the flatbeds. Once we finished at the railhead, we headed back to the camp. The first thing we would do in the morning was take down the tents.

Early in the following day, we didn't need the first call; most of us couldn't wait to return to Ray Barracks and get back to everyday life. We had a box lunch for our breakfast. We cleaned all around our camping area, ensuring nothing was left behind.

In the afternoon, we had a company meeting and were informed about our trip back to Friedberg. We had about one hour before the trucks taking us to the Bahnhof a few miles away would arrive—just enough time to purchase something at the temporary PX store. There's nothing like getting a few snacks to take with us on the overnight trip back.

Chapter Twenty-One
Getting Together with My Twin

Arriving back at the Barracks early in the morning after the long overnight train ride from the Grafenwöhr training area was exhausting. It had been several weeks since Gil arrived in Frankfurt, and it was about time we got together.

Getting back from field problems is always busy, as we knew there would be inspections in the barracks and the motor pool. Every morning, I had to shave, whether I needed it or not, rushing to the bathroom and then to the shower. I returned to the room to get dressed, straighten up my area, make the bed, sweep the floor, and pick up anything that didn't belong.

Reveille sounded off, and we all headed out to the company formation. Everyone was present and accounted for; nobody had snuck out the night before. I went to the orderly room to apply for an overnight pass to visit my brother in Frankfurt that evening. After applying for the pass, I ate breakfast with my squad in the back of the mess hall.

I told the guys I would be going to Frankfort after work. Hearing me mention it, Neil, who was sitting at the table nearby, asked if he could join me. He'd go his way once in Frankfort and later meet me back at the Bahnhof at 2200 hours. I told Neil I didn't mind; Neil wanted to check out a few nightclubs.

After breakfast, I returned to the room to make sure everything was in order. I also had to sweep the hallway, as it was my responsibility. I nearly finished my job in the room and hallway, and then we were back in formation for a work call. All the drivers were to report to the motor pool to work on the vehicles, wash them and top them off.

I always enjoyed working on the track. I started the engine and opened all the hatches—there were three in total—and dropped the back ramp. The rest of the day was spent cleaning: stripping the track, removing everything, and washing the inside to get rid of all the mess left behind by the team. I even removed the floorboards to make sure the sump pumps were free of debris and in good working order.

During break time, one of the drivers from our platoon would stay at the motor pool, and the rest would go to the PX snack bar. I didn't mind going to the snack bar because that little tramp who gave me the clap was no longer working there. After leaving the snack bar, I went to the company orderly room to call Gil to let him know we were back from the field and that I would be coming to Frankfurt to meet him after work. Gil was as excited as I was to be together after a year and a half apart. He told me he would not be able to get a pass to go to town, but there was plenty to do on the base.

Back at the motor pool, I continued working on the track, putting everything back in place and driving it to the wash racks for a good cleaning. Afterward, I went to the gas pumps to top off the track. The track had a 180-gallon capacity and a range of about 300 miles on the road. Back in my parking spot in the motor pool, I wanted to touch up the track as there were a few scratches from running through the woods and hitting trees. I went to the maintenance shop to get some paint to touch up. That didn't take long, and as always, I love having a clean track.

Around 1630 hours, I stayed in the motor pool. I didn't have to make the radio communication formation, as Sergeant Downs knew the drivers were already there. We did our daily radio checks, and all was good. Then, we went back to the barracks as the workday was over.

That day, I skipped dinner because I wanted to leave as soon as possible. Neil felt the same way—he was just as ready as I was. Once at the train station, we didn't have to wait long, as the train to the big city of Frankfurt came by every fifteen minutes. Once in Frankfurt, Neil and I separated after making plans to meet at the station at 2200 hours. I would take the underground as far as the General Hospital, then wait for bus number 63. Bus 63 ran right in front of the Kaserne off Hamburger Strasse. Gil had given me great directions.

Walking through the front gate, I showed the Unit Police my military ID, and he let me through the gate. It was the very first building on the left of the Guard Shack. I reported to the orderly room and asked for Roy, and one of the runners went to get him. Gil came from his room still in his work clothes. He asked if I was hungry, and I told him I hadn't eaten yet. We went to the EM club for an early dinner. While having dinner, Gil said he had asked for a pass since I was visiting and that I knew my way around Frankfurt. His boss was a Colonel, which overrode the company commander, and Gil was approved a pass for the evening.

After eating, we went to his room so he could clean up, and we headed to town. We took the same route I had taken to get to the Kaserne: bus number 63 to the hospital, then the subway to the city center, where there was a shopping center for US families. Not far from there was an American nightclub called The Topper Club. Once in the club, I saw a couple of friends from the base sitting and asked us to sit with them.

The Topper Club was one of the best clubs in Frankfurt for the military personnel to enjoy. It was a safe place; most club members were military personnel off duty, with some military spouses and dependents as well. Live entertainment was featured every Friday and Saturday evening. While at this club, we didn't have to worry about being tricked by some scam artist. We'd meet some lovely ladies who were military dependents. One problem, though, was you didn't want to date one of these girls if their parents were officers in our unit; that wouldn't pass too well.

We stayed at the Topper Club for about an hour, and after a couple of drinks, we decided to head down to Kaiser Strasse. Kaiser Strasse was known as the most sinful street in Germany, with more prostitutes on this street than you could imagine. These so-called working girls were legal and had to undergo monthly medical checks. This time, one of my friends we met downtown, Roberts, wanted to visit one of these beautiful women. On Kaiser Strasse, the girls were expensive. Roberts had the cash, and he always bargained the price down. He had told Gil and me he was going with a woman and would return in about half an hour. Across the street was a sidewalk café. Gil and I went to sit, and, as you'd expect it, we ordered a beer. By the time Roberts returned, we had finished our drinks and were ready to head to the nearby train station.

Gill asked Roberts how it was, and Roberts, a joker, told us what went on for the half hour he was with this fine-looking woman. He went on to say she enjoyed placing food on him and eating it right off him. Then he told us she had him lie down on the bed naked and brought his manhood hard, and placed a pineapple slice on his manhood, put whipped cream over it, and topped it off with a cherry. Roberts said it looked so delicious he nearly ate it himself. She went down on Roberts, and as he told us, we laughed. Well, Roberts told us the hooker ate it all and licked him clean. We were still laughing, but Roberts went on and told us she took a condom out of her purse and rolled it down on his manhood. He then told us she got on top of him and slid down to finish with him, getting off with just a few strokes.

As we started toward the train station, Roberts told us the hooker doesn't get on the bottom as most of the hookers in Frankfurt take great care of their hair. Remember the '60s; the girls liked to place their hair up to resemble a beehive.

We arrived at the train station. I saw Neal on the hardstand waiting for the train. We boarded the train. Then Gil and Roberts went toward the underground, and that was the first night we spent together in Frankfurt, Germany. I was back in Friedberg in about 45 minutes; being this late, Neil and I took a cab back to the base.

Chapter Twenty-Two
Alert War Games

It was 0300 hours, and the sirens sounded across the base and throughout the Friedberg area. Here we go again—I jumped out of bed and dressed for another fun day. When an alert sounded, we didn't know if it was just on the post to see how fast and ready we were, or if it would take us away for a day or a few days. We always kept our backpacks equipped with clean underwear and one change of work clothes. I threw that bag over my shoulder, and off I went.

Hurriedly, we left for the arms room for our weapons, which included the fifty-caliber machine gun and tripod. Most of us were between 18 and 25, so being young was an adventure. Something we would be able to tell our children and later to our grandchildren, maybe even write about it.

At the motor pool, I was not the first one there. The sounds of all those army vehicles made it difficult to hear each other without yelling and shouting. We set down the 50-caliber machine gun, and I climbed onto the track, unlocked the driver's hatch, and climbed in. I started the vehicle and dropped the rear ramp to let the rest of the team to do their part. The 50-caliber machine gun was at its base at the Track Commander's hatch. I put the radios on to verify our communication and see if our radios were functioning correctly. Only two of us had radio communication on the track: the track commander, Sargent

Downs, and I. The next thing I heard over the headset was, okay, specialist raised the ramp and followed the rest of the platoon. In revving up the engine, I accelerated, and off we started to move. We headed toward the back gate; I knew we would move off base and didn't know how long we'd be gone.

We drove on small and narrow streets; this is the part I didn't like about going to these small streets. Sometimes, we'd have to run one of my tracks on the street and the other on the sidewalk, thus destroying their beautiful roadwork. These Germans took pride in their work, and we'd drive through their little villages, and it was like a storm ripping through their small town. One day, I saw a couple of workers placing cobblestones on a sidewalk. When they saw me coming down the narrow street, they just stepped back and sat on the ground near a case of warm beer and drank away.

While driving on a farm road, I noticed three little children waving their hands toward the track, so I slowed down. The children raised their hands toward me as if begging for food. Layton broke open a case of rations and started to hand out some of the canned goods, but that's not what they wanted. They pointed to their lips as if they were smoking; Layton threw some C-ration cigarettes. That's what the little ones wanted. Driving a little further, I saw a cow in a second-floor window. I had to ask Sergeant Downs over the headset why a cow was in their house. The sergeant told me it was a way to keep their home warm. And we think we had it challenging at times.

Sergeant Downs instructed me to enter a tote road that would lead us to the tree line about half a mile from the main road with a suitable place to camp out for the night or until told to change our position. The Sergeant called in our point to the mess truck, which we might not even see. That meant we would have to eat cold C-rations, which were not too tasty, but we had to do with what we had.

At this point, there were 7 of us on this track. It was getting a little bit cold, so we kept the track buttoned down to keep the inside of the track on the warm side. We'd take turns staying on watch; Layton and I went on the lookout for two hours while the others remained on the track and tried to get some rest and sleep. We walked the tree line for about a mile. I had a walkie-talkie to keep in touch with the rest of the team. A narrow tote road was at the end of the tree line; Layton wanted us to follow the road leading to this tiny little village. I had an idea Layton was hoping to find a place where he could buy some beer. By this time, you probably guessed Layton had an alcohol use disorder. I swear he could smell a Gasthaus a mile away. As we walked downhill toward the village, we came upon a few houses, and sure enough, there was a Gasthaus in that little cluster of buildings.

Layton handed me his weapons and helmet, entered the Gasthaus, and bought four beers to drink on our way back to camp. He paid less than a dollar for the beers, which was a great deal; that would have cost at least twice that much in Friedberg. When Layton showed up, he handed me a beer, and I returned his equipment. Then, we headed back to the camp. It took us a little longer to return to our campsite; all was quiet in radio communication with Sergeant Downs. We arrived at the camp, and everybody was inside the track resting. Sergeant Downs wanted us to pitch up tents for the night but then decided we'd be better off sleeping in a warm track, and if called to move position, we'd be ready. I slept in the driver's seat, the most comfortable place in the track. Occasionally, I would have to start the track so I could turn on the heater to warm the inside of the track.

An hour had passed, and it was somewhat chilly, so I started the track and turned on the heater. While the track was running, I went out for a smoke. Sergeant Downs saw I was out, so he came out with me, and we talked for a long time. The Sergeant said he was happy with my work and how I responded to all my duties. He asked me if I'd be interested in becoming the squad leader as he would become the platoon leader, taking over Sergeant Bundy's position. I was honored and told him I would be interested in the job. He told me that when we returned to the company, he would announce to the platoon members that I would become the squad leader. I would also have a temporary Sergeant position until I went to the NCO (Non-Commissioned Officer) Academy.

This information was exciting news for me. Sargent Downs did ask me to keep this quiet. I told him I was due for a vacation when we returned to the barracks, and I didn't want to miss out on this trip as it was the main reason I joined the Army. Not to worry, he told me it would be a few months before I would be sent to the NCO Academy as there was a waiting list to get in.

We went back to the track to get some rest. I shut off the heater and did the same to the track. The night seemed to have gone by fast after I fell asleep. I woke up after hearing someone calling on the radio; the mess truck was looking for our location. I gave them our location, and they told me they should be at our location within an hour. During this morning, everyone had to go out to relieve themselves. Therefore, we each were issued an entrenching tool. We had to take a dump in the woods, we had to dig a hole, and when we finished, we had to bury the hole.

The mess truck showed up a little late; there was nothing like fake eggs for breakfast, which was gross. After breakfast, we all stayed outside of the track. While the squad members were out of the vehicle, I took a few minutes to straighten out the track. I checked to see how much fuel I had left in the tank; I could use more gas as I was below half a tank. After I told the Sergeant we were below half a gas tank, Sergeant Downs called for a fuel delivery truck. Sergeant Downs told me the fuel truck would arrive at this location within an hour.

The fuel truck arrived; I climbed on the track as the gas outlet was on top. I removed the gas cap and installed the nozzle into the gas tank opening. After pumping at least one hundred gallons of gas, I removed the nozzle from the tank opening. The nozzle slipped from my hands and spewed a little gas on my face and eyes. I jumped off the track and rolled on the ground as if I was on a small knoll. When I stopped moving, I grabbed my canteen of water and poured water over my face and eyes. Sergeant Downs called for the medic to attend to me. It took about twenty minutes before the medics showed up. I was feeling better while waiting for the medics to show up. I kept on flushing my eyes, which the medic said I did well; all was good, and there were no restrictions as far as my eyes. It was okay for me to keep on driving when I had to.

Later that afternoon, Sergeant Downs met us briefly to inform us about our next move. I drove the track around the little village we were watching. Half of the squad stayed at the campsite with Sergeant Downs. We kept in touch with each other with our two-way radios. We did have maps of the area and used them to map our way around the small village. Off we went, and Layton was acting as the track commander. We drove through the forest on tote roads and saw beautiful views through the woods. I pulled up next to a small Gasthaus and held the position until Sergeant Downs called for us back to the campsite.

He ordered us to return to the campsite; the truck was present with our meals. After we had eaten, we had another short meeting to discuss what we would be doing for the second night at this campsite. We agreed we would be able to sleep in the track again tonight. We were to take turns on watch duty, two teams designated at two-hour intervals. Layton and I were on the same team; as I said earlier, Layton was good and served in Vietnam like King did a couple of times.

If I went with Layton, we'd end up at the same Gasthaus for a few beers and some good German food. Layton and I took the 2000 hours to 2200 hours watch. At about 19:30 hours, Layton and I started getting our gear together to go when the other team arrived. On this mission, we had the walkie-talkie; for weapons, all we took with us was our sidearm. Off we went, but just before leaving, Sergeant Downs told us he didn't want to see us bring any beer back from the recon mission.

Layton and I left, and it was starting to get dark. We must have walked about 2 miles, which took us about forty-five minutes to reach the small village. Approaching a Gasthaus, we noticed outside seating with an enclosure around it, which was good for us. This way, if Sergeant Downs asked us if we went into any Gasthaus, we could say no and tell the truth. We sat outside at one of the tables, and of course, this drew a little attention from some passersby. A young waitress came to the table and greeted us; she took our orders because Layton and I wanted some well-cooked food. The waitress soon returned with our beer and told us our meal would be out in a few minutes. As we sat there drinking our beer, we noticed the tables around us started to get filled up by some locals. Not because of the food but because Layton and I were all dressed in combat uniforms; I guess that would attract people's attention. Our food orders came, and they sure looked very delicious. We ordered Wienerschnitzel with potato salad, and it was delicious.

After we had eaten, the waitress came and asked if she could sit with us. No problem there, I just pulled a chair for her, and she sat with us. She was Marie, and she told us her father owned the Gasthaus. He was happy that we stopped at his business for dinner as it attracted people to have dinner here because of us and that her father said the beer was on him.

Marie asked what we were doing in this little village, and we told her we were camping in the wood line. Her father came to see us just before we left to thank us for our business. We were welcomed to his Gasthaus anytime we were in town. We paid the bill, shook hands with the owner, and left.

It was dark out, so Layton and I walked somewhat faster than we did when we left camp. We might have been about halfway back to camp when we received a call on the walkie-talkie from Sergeant Downs. He told us to get moving faster as it was dark, and he didn't want us to get lost. We were forbidden from using lights or smoking as a light source that could give our position away.

Arriving at camp, Sergeant Downs wanted me to move the track to a different location, which was my job. This time, he wanted the rest of the squad to walk on the tote road behind, using the track as cover. We moved about a mile toward the village, the same direction Laton and I came from. Again, we slept inside the track that night. There had to be at least one person to staff the radio, and we took a one-hour shift on radio watch.

Waking up in the morning, we were getting to the point where we had to get cleaned. It's been nearly three days since we've seen the inside of a shower room. There was a five-gallon can of water, so we made a small campfire to heat water and shave and wash up the best we could with what we had. We used our helmets to put water in and then placed them over the fire to heat the water. Within an hour, we had all gotten cleaned. I got on the radio to find out when the mess truck would arrive. What I got for a reply wasn't what I expected. I discovered the mess truck broke down about three miles away on the main road.

I started up the track, raised the rear ramp, and headed toward the mess truck. We got there in about 15 minutes—same old breakfast: powdered eggs and sausage with soggy toast. The food was terrible when out in the field. Sure, I'm glad I got to eat a good dinner the night before at the Gasthaus.

After breakfast, Sergeant Downs was on the radio. When he finished talking to the person on the other end, we gathered, and he informed us the game was over and we would head back to Friedberg.

We waited for our company's other vehicles as we continued to Friedberg in a convoy. We must have traveled about three hours before returning to the base. When we arrived, we headed to the motor pool, and from there, the team started to carry their personal belongings to the squad room. As for me, I had a job to do that was on my track. Layton returned to the track to help me carry the 50-caliber machine gun back to the arms room where Rhea was working. After we checked our weapons with Rhea, the arms room personnel, I returned to the motor pool to get the track cleaned. After a couple of hours, I stopped for the day.

Chapter Twenty-Three
England

For over a year and a half, I've been waiting for this day—the main reason I joined the Army for four years. Finally, I would meet my pen-pal, Gail, from Bolton, England. I met Gail by listening to a Boston, Mass., W.L.B.Z. radio station. I had been listening to the radio station back in 1964. On Saturday mornings, the station would announce the names of people looking for pen pals in America. When I heard Gail's name and that she was from England, I wanted to write to anyone from England. I figured she would get many letters from people in the States replying to this request, so I had to write to ensure Gail would not let my letter go by the wayside.

I don't remember what the whole letter was about, but I wanted it to stand out when I wrote to Gail. After a couple of weeks, when I received a reply from Gail, I knew it would work—unless my letter was the only one she had received. I'll reveal my secret: When I wrote the letter to Gail, I wrote every other word in cursive and printed the others. We became exceptionally good pen-pals; even today, after 50 years, we are still in touch with each other.

My flight was leaving Frankfurt Flughafen/Airport on Monday morning. I had another day before my two weeks' leave to start. On Sunday, before my departure, I took an overnight pass and went to Frankfurt to see my brother Gil.

I left Friedberg after lunch to go to the Bahnhof to catch a train to Frankfurt. I enjoyed taking the train to Frankfurt. The views were outstanding. There must have been about seven stops between Friedberg and Frankfurt. At the road crossings, I'd look out the window and see the cars and trucks stop to allow the train to pass. At times, I would also see people standing at the crossing. It seemed people weren't in a hurry, and the Germans were genuinely lovely.

Getting off the train, I headed toward the main entrance to the station. Across the street from the Main entrance was Kaiser Strasse, one of the most sinful streets in Germany. I thought I'd walk to the General Hospital and then take bus number 63 to the Kaserne, where Gil lived. I would have to cross the trolley tracks to get to Kaiser Strasse; there is an underground crossway to the other side. As I went to travel underground, I stopped to use the men's room. As I was standing at the urinal, a bunch of business cards was on a rack. The cards were advertising for call girls, with a picture of a girl and a phone number. I took one, as I wanted to show some of the guys. Three hookers approached me before I arrived at the hospital. I did ask how much it cost, and each was different. The closer to the city center, the more expensive they were.

Finally, I arrived at Gil's barracks, where he was waiting for me. We went to the club on the post, and as we walked into the club, we saw a few slot machines next to the men's room. Gil and I went to a table, sat down, and ordered something to drink. I got up to go to the men's room and decided to play the twenty-five cents slot machine on my way out of the men's room. After several pulls of the one-arm bandit, I deposited more money in the slot machine and hit a jackpot of seventy-five dollars. The manager had me sign for the winnings and then told me to put another quarter in the machine to run off the winning jackpot. Holy shit, I had hit another jackpot—damn, I've never heard of that before. I put another quarter in the machine and unbelievably hit a third jackpot for the third time. This time, he would not let me play it off; instead, he put the machine out of order. The extra two hundred and twenty-five dollars made my journey to England easier and more enjoyable, knowing I had enough money to have a great time.

I returned to Gil's table and told him about my luck at the slot machines. After finishing our drinks, we went to town for some live entertainment. We went to the Topper Club, which became Gil's and my favorite. I liked the Topper Club as it seemed safer than the clubs in the city. Most of the patrons at this place were Americans. I told Gil about my plans to attend the NCO Academy, and he said that was an innovative idea. It was time for me to go back to Friedberg for the night.

Gil and I parted ways here at the club. He returned to his barracks, and I headed out to catch the subway back to the Bahnhof for the train ride to Friedberg. I got back to my barracks around 2300 hours. I went to the supply room to retrieve my travel suitcase the following day. That's right, it's the same suitcase I purchased to go to the World's Fair with. Starting my leave, I was exempt from any formations, so I packed my bag and went to the mess hall for breakfast.

After breakfast, I went to the orderly room and signed up for two weeks in England. I went to tell the guys that I would see them in two weeks and for them to have an exciting time while I was gone. Sergeant Downs was to take over my track while I was gone. Sergeant Downs gave me a ride to the front gate, and I took a cab. I told the cab driver I was going to the train station in town, and it took about five minutes to drive there. Trains are always on time; I wasn't at the station for five minutes, the train arrived, and I was on my way. I was extremely excited to finally be on my way to England. I've been dreaming about this trip for quite a while now. Arriving at Frankfurt Bahnhof, I hired a cab to take me to the airport. This cab driver took me the long way around the airport. When arriving at the airport, the cab driver asked for more money than the trip cost. I told him I was only paying half of what he requested; he wondered why I wouldn't pay the bill. I told him I had lived in the area for almost two years, and he took me for a joy ride before getting to the airport. He agreed he took me for a ride, and I only paid him half the fare he demanded.

My flight was going to be on British Airlines, which was my choice of airplane at the time. I walked to the departing gate, found a place to sit, and waited for the flight to London. In the last month, Gail and I communicated via postal mail to get information about how I would get to find where they lived. I was going from the airport to Victoria Station in London and taking the train to Bolton. Gail's dad would pick me up at the station in Bolton. I told Gail I would be hauling a blue suitcase with red stripes across my suitcase.

I heard an announcement over the PA system that my flight was arriving. We should be boarding soon; please approach the gate. I noticed people were coming to the gate. The area was filling up; I'm glad I had an assigned seat. The doors opened, people started walking out of the plane, and the people in the waiting area lined up to get ready to board.

Once on the plane, I found my assigned seat at a window seat. It took about an hour and a half before the plane landed in London. Once in London, I went through customs and was on the streets quickly. Hailing down a cab wasn't hard at all. One cab stopped; I threw my bags in the back seat, and off we went to Victoria Station. Victory Station is an excellent station; there were even pubs there. I went to purchase a ticket to Bolton. The teller was a lady, and she told me she loved my accent. I thought everybody had an accent and not me. I bought my ticket, and I had an hour before my train left. I went across the way and into a pub. I drank a few beers and forgot about the train until I heard the PA announcements. I headed out with my bag, and the train pulled away when I got to the tracks.

I went to the ticket window to find out when the next train to Bolton was coming and was then informed the next train to Bolton would be in about three hours. This time, I just went on the platform and sat on a bench; I wouldn't miss the next train. It was about two and a half hours, and there was still no train. I went to the ticket window and asked about the train. The girl told me God saved me, and I wondered what she meant. The lady said the train I missed went off track. The next train will be on a different track in five minutes. At this time, I called Gail to let her know that I would arrive later because of the train derailment. By the time I arrived at the platform, the train was coming. This train ride would take about three hours to get to Bolton.

When arriving in Bolton, I got off the train and headed out to the street, and hopefully, Gail's dad was waiting. I stood in one place and put my bag in front of me so Gail's dad could see the red stripes. I heard my name, and it was Gail's dad. We shook hands and greeted each other. Mister Bond was the only one to meet me at the station. Sitting on the left side of the car as a passenger felt weird. It did not take too long to arrive at the house. Gail lived in a smaller town just a few miles away.

Gail and her mother were outside waiting for us to arrive. Gail walked toward me to give me a warm hug, and I also gave her a warm hug in return. Meeting Gail's family made me feel at home with friends. Mister Bond took my bag into their home, and I followed him to an upstairs bedroom. He told me this was his son's bedroom and that he would stay at a friend's house during my stay. We went back downstairs to where Gail and her mother were. We sat in the front room and had some Tea. We sat for a couple of hours, exchanging each other's questions. Gail was still attending school, so the next day, I was to spend some time at the fire station as Mister Bond was a firefighter.

After a while, Gail's mother called us into the dining room for dinner. I have never eaten Brussels Sprouts until now. I have never heard of Yorkshire Pudding before this day. The food was great, and I love trying new foods I have never eaten. After dinner, Mister Bond and I went to the front room and talked until the ladies came to sit with us. Gail and I sat on the sofa with her mother, and Mister Bond sat in a lounge chair. We watched television for a while and then gave in for the night. We said our good nights and got up to bed for the night.

I got up early the following day. Mrs. Bond had breakfast ready on the table. Gail and Mr. Bond were already in the breakfast room having their breakfast. Mr. Bond asked if I would spend time with him at the Fire Station where he was employed. I told him I was ready and looking forward to meeting his co-workers and checking out his workplace. He worked at the fire station in the next town, Bolton, about six miles away. After breakfast, Mr. Bond and I left for the station after we said our goodbyes to the girls. I hoped to spend time with Gail but did not want to disappoint her father.

Driving through these narrow streets differed from driving on the wide roads in the States. We arrived at the fire station, and it seemed as if the people working at the station were expecting me. Mister Bond introduced me to some of the people working at the station. After meeting some of the people, they stopped for a small break for some tea. At the station, there was a full kitchen with a cook. I'm not a tea drinker, so I asked if they had coffee; all they had was instant coffee. The instant coffee would be fine; I poured a cup, and all the others had tea. The fire station was near the village, and Mr. Bond had to leave the station on this call.

I stayed behind and went for a walk through the village. I visited a few small shops and wanted to see what products sold in these small markets. Things were vastly different from the stores in the States. I went into a supermarket and looked at several types of products. While I was looking around, one of the employees asked me if she could help. I asked her about the various kinds of products on the shelves. The lady may have been about five years older than I, and she looked at me and said she loved my accent. She then asked where I was from. I told her I was from Maine, USA. She wasn't sure exactly where that was, so I explained that it was about 200 miles north of Boston, Mass.

Excited, this lady called a couple of her co-workers to meet me. Of course, they were girls, and they enjoyed talking with me. They asked me where I was from and why I was in Bolton. One of the girls about my age asked if I wanted to go out for lunch with her; she was a beautiful young lady. I told this young lady I had plans the whole time I visited the area. She offered to give me her mailing address so we could write. Still, I told her that I was in the US Army and was remarkably busy writing letters to friends and family. After a while, I returned to the fire station to meet up with Mr. Bond again. The fire crew that had left earlier was back from their call. We sat down at a table, and some had lunch. They had an excellent cook, and the prepared food was outstanding. After lunch, everybody helped to clean up the dining area.

There was a pool table at the fire station, and we played a few games. The table was a little different than the ones I used to play on at home. This table was much larger; it only had solid color balls and no pockets on the table. I learned a new game; it was fun, and the time passed.

Mr. Bond's shift was over, and it was time to go home, but first, he had to stop at the market to pick up a few things for Mrs. Bond to help her finish what she was making for dinner. The market we went to was like a farmers' market; there were all these little food stands, and other kinds of wares people were selling. It was different from the shopping I used to do at home in the States. When we arrived at the house, Gail had a couple of friends with her, and Mrs. Bond was preparing dinner. Sitting in the front room, Gail introduced me to her friends; the girl was her classmate, and the boy was from Spain. We talked while Mrs. Bond was preparing dinner, and the food smelled great.

Gail informed me she, the other couple, and I were going to a nightclub in Manchester called Tiffany's. We got to know each other better by discussing our everyday lives and activities. A boy from Spain was visiting Gail's friend as they were old friends. After dinner, Mr. Bond asked if I wanted to drive his car to Manchester. I declined because I didn't dare drive on the left side of the road. He understood what I was saying, so Mr. Bond would be the person to drive us to the Manchester nightclub. We left at about 1930 hours, which was 7:30 PM, and the drive to Manchester was about twenty minutes. Once at the club, we went in, and there was a small cover charge. I paid for Gail, and the other couple paid their way in. At first, Gail insisted she pay her way, but I told her the boys paid for their dates at home.

We found a place where the four of us could sit together. Once we sat down, the server came for our order. I bought a round for the four of us. There was live entertainment that evening; the group who played there was from the States. They had a few records out at this time. Gail and I danced; I was a complete gentleman in the present with Gail. She was a beautiful and caring girl. I never tried to over-advance her; my dad taught me better.

After a couple of dances, we went back to the table. This time, when the server came to the table to see if we wanted another drink, we all ordered. When the server returned with our drinks, I noticed everyone had reached to pay for their drinks. I motioned the server over and paid for the second round of drinks. After a short while, we left the club and walked further down the street. We passed a radio and television station, and Gail's friend said it would be nice to go inside it to check the place out. What's stopping us from going in? I asked. We can always tell them I'm a recording artist star from America, and that's what we did, and they gave us a tour of the station. We had a wonderful time there, and the tour was awe-inspiring.

We returned to the street and headed back toward the club, as Gail's father would return to pick us up soon. When we arrived outside Tiffany's nightclub, her dad awaited us. We got into the car and headed back to the house. Mr. Bond took the other two kids home first. When we arrived at Gail's, her mother had tea and coffee ready for us. These people were friendly and treated me like they had known me for years.

As we sat in the front room watching the television, we talked about what we would do for the next day. Gail's dad had the next day off, and Gail was taking a day off so the four of us could have a day as a holiday. We planned to go to the city of Blackpool, but first, we would drive through Liverpool and in the neighborhood where the group "The Beatles" was raised. Liverpool was about an hour's drive away.

Chapter Twenty-Four
Holiday To the Coast

Waking up the next morning felt like a fantastic day for a day trip to the coast. The sun was shining, and not too many clouds in the sky. I got out of bed, and the bathroom was accessible, so I went in, shaved, and dressed for the day. It was going to be a little chilly out by the ocean, so I did have a light jacket that I had brought along. Mr. Bond drove, I sat in the passenger seat, and Mrs. Bond and Gail sat in the back seat. About an hour and fifteen minutes later, we arrived in Liverpool. We drove through a few neighborhoods where the Beatles lived, and it was a little exciting for me as the Beatles were my favorite singing group.

After touring Liverpool, we headed to Blackpool for lunch. Blackpool was a city on the west coast of England. This place reminded me of Revere Beach in Massachusetts, with many amusements, rides, the beach across the street, and many friendly people. We went to the Blackpool Tower; this was where we had our lunch. It was the first time I'd ever been up in a tower of this kind; it resembled the Eiffel Tower. I don't quite remember what I ate, but I remember having a Double Diamond beer, another first.

Talking with Gail and her parents, I told the Bonds that I had to prepare to attend the NCO Academy. Mr. Bond asked if I would make the Army my life—not really, not knowing I wanted to spend twenty-some years in the Army. I didn't tell them I enlisted in the Army mainly to meet Gail. I didn't want Gail to feel any obligation to me. When lunch was over, we left the tower, took a walk on the boardwalk, and then headed back to their house. The drive back to Bury was enjoyable. Gail and I sat in the back seat together. Gail and I talked about how we should get to know each other better.

When we returned to their house, Mrs. Bond made some sandwiches as a light dinner. Gail had to go places alone a few times, like dancing lessons. Other times, she didn't come home from school because she would be working at school after hours. Later, I found out that Gail had a steady boyfriend. Her mom and I talked after Gail went to bed since she had to get up for school. Mrs. Bond also told me that when Gail placed that ad at WLBZ, a Boston radio station, she received over three hundred letters. Gail gave some of the letters to her classmates but kept my letter.

During the next few days, I'd walk to the center of the village to pass the time. I was told that Gail was in dance classes and spent much time with her boyfriend afterward. She lied to me, and that will always stay with me. Had she told me she was seeing someone, I might have never taken leave to visit England. Looking at it differently, I did visit England, and in my way, I had an enjoyable time.

A few days later, I walked into the village and sat in a pub for a few beers. This one time, I left the pub and walked back to the house to find a person at home with Mrs. Bond visiting. The person was a news reporter doing a story on Gail and me—an American pen pal visiting England. As I write this paragraph, I'm just figuring out why she didn't want any pictures of the two of us together. It had to be because she had a steady boyfriend. Her mother never took out a camera, and there was never a picture of Gail and me simultaneously. Now, I think that was very weird.

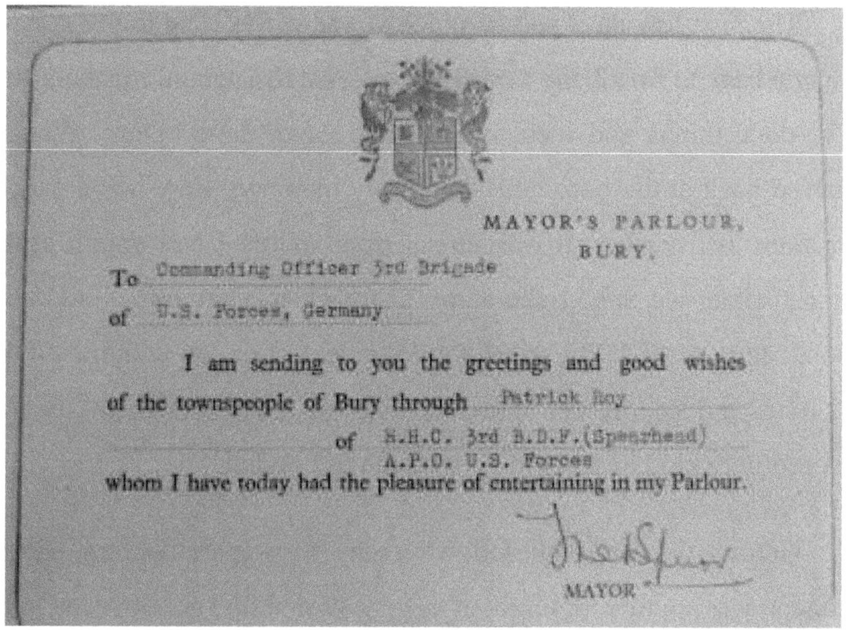

MAYOR'S PARLOUR,
BURY.

To Commanding Officer 3rd Brigade

of U.S. Forces, Germany

I am sending to you the greetings and good wishes of the townspeople of Bury through Patrick Roy

of H.H.C. 3rd B.D.F.(Spearhead)
A.P.O. U.S. Forces

whom I have today had the pleasure of entertaining in my Parlour.

MAYOR

As a Goodwill Ambassador, Gail's aunt had arranged for me to go to the mayor's office. I met the city's mayor and had tea while talking for about an hour. The mayor gave me the Key to the City for a day. He asked me what I would enjoy doing while I had the Key. I told him I would be highly interested in visiting the law courts. I was to arrive at the courthouse the following day, and someone would meet me there. The person would show me around, and he would be my guide.

We sat in the courthouse, and I found it remarkably interesting. The judge and the lawyer wore long black gowns and had those wigs on their heads. I enjoyed the day in the courthouse. When I left, I started walking back to the house. I stopped at a pharmacy on my way back, as I had an upset stomach and needed something to calm it down.

The next few days passed quickly, and it was time to prepare for my trip back to Friedberg. I must say my visit to England was fantastic. I've done things and seen things I had never done before. When I arrived back at the house, all the family members were home except for Sam, her brother. It was dinner time. While I was sitting at the dinner table, we talked about my trip back to Germany. Gail, Mrs. Bond, and one of Gail's aunts would travel to London with me on the train instead of my returning to London alone. I thought it was exceedingly kind of them to go with me to London.

Getting up early the following day to prepare for our trip to London was another highlight of this vacation. I said goodbye to Gail's father as he was going to work at the fire station. It wasn't more than a few minutes before Gail's aunt arrived with her car. I packed my bag, and they were ready to be taken to the car. I took my bag to the vehicle and placed it in its trunk.

Once at the train station, I took the bag from the trunk. Mrs. Bond opened the doors to the station, and we all entered. They went to the ticket window to buy tickets. I already had my return ticket to London. We boarded the train and found a place for all four to sit together. I placed my bag above on a rack; this was a compartment car, so we had our compartment for the four of us. Gail's aunt was a reporter, which may have had something to do with me visiting the Mayor's Chambers.

After a couple of hours of talking, I asked if anybody would like something as I would go to the dining car. We all wanted a small snack because when we got to London, we would have several hours before going to Heathrow Airport. Gail and I walked about eight cars before arriving in the dining car at the food counter to order our food. Gail told me that this trip to London was her first time in London. I placed the food order; it took a few minutes before the order was ready, then Gail carried the drinks, and I carried the food back. Back in the compartment, we sat and enjoyed our meal. Mrs. Bond asked how much the food was, and I said it was on me and it was my pleasure.

Arriving at Victoria Station, I took the bag, got off the train, and headed for the streets. It was lunchtime, and we saw several outside cafes and then sat at one of the tables. We all ordered something to drink the ladies, and Gail ordered tea, and I ordered a beer. It was a beautiful day in the City of London, and it was the same for every city I have visited in Europe; I loved it. I sat at the beauty of the day, enjoying the view of the traffic and the people going by. We were less than a block away from Piccadilly Circus. The waiter came with the bill, and I told him I would take it—the four meals cost just under a five-dollar note in US money. I left two American quarters on the table as a tip. Mrs. Bond reached over and took the two quarters, and I asked what she was doing. She did replace it with British coins. She told me she wanted the coins as souvenirs, so I reached into my pocket and found a few more USA coins for her.

It was time for us to leave each other. I hugged Gail's mother and hugged Gail. Then I turned around and headed out, never seeing her again while in the Army. I jumped on the bus, not looking back, sitting down as it drove off. It took about thirty minutes to get to the airport. I stepped off the bus and walked toward the building entrance, customs, and then the gate where the flight would take off. I boarded the airplane, and within a few minutes, the airplane took off into the sky. I was leaving Heathrow Airport and arriving at Frankfurt Airport in less than two hours. After passing through customs, I headed outside to hail a cab. I ordered the driver to take me to the nearest underground transport station.

Chapter Twenty-Five

The Academy

Back in Frankfurt, I went to Division HQ to see Gil at work and let him know I was back from England. Gil was getting off work when I arrived. He did not expect me, as I wanted to surprise him. I had to wait in the orderly room until Gil returned to the barracks. When he walked by, I called him, and he stopped. I asked if I could still stay the night in his room on the weekend. I didn't have to be back in Friedberg until 0700 hours on Monday. He said I'd have to sleep in the sleeping bag; it's no big deal here. Gil and I spent the weekend together, and we went downtown after he clocked out. We hit a few nightclubs and even took the time to see a movie there. I don't remember what it was about because it was in German. We didn't stay for the whole movie. We went back to base and hit the bowling alley.

When I returned to the Barracks the following Monday, Sergeant Downs showed up and wanted to talk with me about the NCO Academy and the possibility of re-enlisting in the Army. We went to the PX snack bar to discuss my future with the Army. Sergeant Downs told me that if I re-enlisted, I would get a re-up bonus of up to $4,000.00, which was a lot of money in the '60s. Then he went on and on about the other benefits if I stayed in the Army. I reflected on the Korean conflict, the Vietnam War, and why I was stationed in Germany during the Cold War. In my mind, I didn't see much of a future in the Army. Sergeant Downs even went as far as to say he would set up a date with his daughter. His daughter was a good-looking girl, two years younger than me. I turned down the offer because I still had over two years left on this enlistment.

The second part of our meeting was about what I had to do to prepare for the Academy. I had two months before I attended, and I had been given a list of things to take with me and what to expect while there.

The night before leaving for the NCO Academy, some of the guys wanted to take me out for a final night with the enlistees. However, I was no longer supposed to hang out with the guys, as I was now an acting Sergeant and a squad leader. When I was assigned Acting Sergeant, I had to give up the job I loved — being a track driver.

There was a strip club we had heard of in Frankfort. Four of us decided to take the twenty-minute train ride to Kaiser Strasse in Frankfort to see live sex acts on stage. One had to be aware of the club's location. I believed it was not in a legally acceptable area.

After the radio communication at the motor pool, the guys met me at the mess hall, where we made plans for the night in Frankfort. You could find anything on the Kaiser Strasse, the most sinful street in Frankfurt, Germany.

After dinner, Layton, Victor, Jones, and I returned to the barracks and prepared for our night out. We wanted to leave soon for a great night in Frankfurt. We went through the back gate, walked to the

Bahnhof, and stopped at the Bahnhof Bar for a quick beer. Layton's girlfriend was working that evening, and he went out back with her for about 20 minutes. When Layton returned, we finished our beer and headed across the street and to the station. The train was about five minutes away. Once on the train, we sat in a compartment and rode until we reached the Frankfurt Bahnhof. Still daylight, we decided to stop first at Storyville on the second floor of a side street downtown. Once Jones and I sat down at a table, Layton and Victor weren't interested in the disco club, so they left. We planned to meet them in a couple of hours at another location near the strip club.

After the two left, we ordered a beer and watched people dance to disco music. I noticed a good-looking girl, maybe in her late teens; I asked her if she wanted to dance with me. She accepted, and we went off to the dance floor. German girls just loved to get involved with us young American soldiers. I guessed it was to find their future in hopes of getting married to one of the Americans. Many people married German girls while stationed in West Germany during the Cold War.

The first dance was to a piece of fast disco music. The next dance was a little slower; we were dancing with our bodies close together and a lot of grinding. After that dance, I asked her if she would join me and a friend at our table. She hesitated for a second or two, said she was here with a girlfriend and wanted to know if she could sit with us. No problem; I returned to the table with Jones and let him know we would have the company of two girls.

Both girls arrived at our table, and we stood up. The girl I was dancing with sat in the booth with me, and the other sat with Jones. The waitress approached the table to see if we wanted to order more drinks. We called for more drinks, and when the drinks came, the girls wanted to pay for them, but we wouldn't even think of letting them pay for their drinks. We could tell these two girls were not hookers. The girls didn't ask for coke on the side, which was a good sign that we would not get ripped off. Talking with these two girls, we discovered they were in their last year at the German high school.

The girl I was with was Carmen, and the other young girl was named Karla. After the second drink, Carmen was all over me, rubbing my body, and she grabbed my hand and shoved it under her blouse. She let me massage her firm breasts as she stroked my manhood until I almost lost it. I said let's have another dance, and I had to stop her as I didn't want to get my pants wet and stained. We returned to the dance floor another time before leaving as we had to meet the other two guys, Layton and Victor.

After the dance, I told Carmen we had to leave; we returned to the table to finish our drinks. Carmen and her friend asked if we would be kind enough to walk them to the bus stop, a block away from Storyville. We did walk the girls to the bus stop, and they insisted we each take twenty Marks from them because their parents would find it suspicious that they went out and didn't spend any money. Jones and I looked at each other and said, "Oh well, we may never see these girls again," so we took the Marks. Twenty Marks was just a little under five dollars.

We headed to the strip joint, where we met Layton and Victor so we could enter the club together. This one club was off the Kaiser Strasse and into an alley. Once we entered the building, we headed to the secret room. Once seated, we got more to drink just before the show started. The doorman locked the door from the inside and outside with a false wall. Two girls appeared on the stage and took all their clothes off; you can imagine what they did for the rest. They did things to each other that I didn't think were allowed. After the girls finished performing, two men appeared on the stage with them.

You guessed it; they did perform sex acts in front of all of us in the room. It was unbelievable. I couldn't believe my own eyes. I never expected something like this; I've Been to other strip clubs where girls would strip, but nothing like what we just saw. We were there for about half an hour; the show was over, the doors were unlocked, and then the lights went on, and all had to leave the place as they would have another show after they had a new audience.

It was getting late, and we started to head back to the Bahnhof to take the train back to Friedberg. When we returned to the Friedberg train station, we went across the street to the Bahnhof Bar and had another beer before walking that mile to the back gate before it closed at midnight.

We were returning to the post just a few minutes before the gate would be locked for the night. The back entrance had a small U.P. (Unit Police) hut, maybe a 6' X 6' square, with just enough room for a chair and a sign-in and sign-out book. The Guard was allowed out of this little booth to stretch when he got cramped up. The barracks were the next building over; we entered the building fast and went to bed.

Chapter Twenty-Six

The Academy

I woke up, dressed, and started packing my bag for the NCO Academy. Reveille sounded off, and we all headed out to the company formation. After roll call, I went for breakfast before the work call. Some of the guys, as usual, went to breakfast, and others went back into the building to finish their business and then returned to the mess hall for breakfast.

Sergeant Bundy offered to drive me to the Academy, which was about thirty miles away. Once he had his business taken off, we headed out on the road. Sergeant Bundy drove the company jeep. It was the first time I was a passenger because I usually did the driving. Sergeant Bundy stopped in Giessen to see someone at the quartermaster. We were there for almost two hours before heading out again, but before we continued, we went to the open mess hall for lunch. We finally arrived at the NCO Academy, driving right up to the building where I unloaded my bags. I would be here for a few weeks to learn more about being a soldier. I signed in at the office and was assigned a room similar to the one in Friedberg. I was in an eight-man room, with a shower at one end of the hall and the lavatory at the other.

I went to the room and met some of the men I would be bunking next to. I wasn't interested in making friends; I was here to learn and pass the course. The program would start the following day, and we would be here for seven weeks. It felt like basic training all over again. We had a footlocker and a wall rack for our clothing and personal care products. We had the diagram of how our footlockers and wall racks should be arranged. For this training, we would go through a lot of bullshit: spit-shine boots, shoes, and clothing had to be pressed and edged for all formations. We were going to train in discipline and learn how to become teachers. We were the Army's future leaders and would train to become the best the Army could be. We'd be pushed to the limit, and not everybody would pass this school.

The rest of the day was spent preparing for what would come; it could be hell for me. My new roommates and I worked on our displays until we got it to the tee. After getting everything in order, I went to the service club for a nice, quiet place to write a few letters. I wrote to Gail in England and a few letters back home to my family and friends. I wrote letters to my mother so she would not contact the Company Commander to see if I was still alive.

I decided to check out the service club after writing my letters. I wanted to check the club out to see what they offered. The club wasn't too far away, maybe half a mile. I checked the bulletin boards to see what they had to offer. There weren't many people there, so I left the service club; I returned to the barracks and met Manny, one of my roommates. Manny and I would become friends, and we helped each other out at the Academy. He and I were the same age, and I don't remember where he told me he was from. Before calling it a night, we ensured all our displays were perfect for inspection. Inspections were to be done in our room several times a day.

The first call came at 0500 hours, and somebody, most likely the CQ runner, was banging on each room's doors and yelling the first call: rise and shine. We got up and hurried to take care of our morning business. We had to wait in line to get to the shower, about fifty of us heading down the hall just in our skivvies to the bathroom or the shower room. No modesty at this camp, taking a dump with no bathroom dividers, the toilets so close together that our butt cheeks almost touched together. Another set of toilet bowls was just a couple of feet across the room. Not only did we touch butts on this side, but we also had to face the others across from us. It was the same in the shower; as the old saying goes, you didn't want to drop the soap. The soap on a string was a big plus for us. Shower heads, about six of them lined up next to each other. If you weren't too careful, you might have bumped into someone else, and it wasn't very comfortable when it happened.

All cleaned and ready for the day, waiting for reveille to sound off. Today was my first day back in school, and I soon discovered this wasn't anything like any other school I'd ever attended. The trumpet sounded, and out we joined the company formation. There was a head count, and all were present and accounted for. We were reunited with the group to attend the mess hall for breakfast. We had to go through the horizontal bars as in basic training at Fort Dix. In the chow line, we had to move two steps at a time and be at parade rest when not moving.

Many drill instructors were close by to watch us—one step out of line and twenty push-ups given as punishment for not following orders.

We had fifteen minutes to eat in the mess hall while in training. We would have the weekends off from training, exempting us from the daily torture, and even allowed a pass to town. While we were at breakfast, we watched closely to avoid making any mistakes. We were prohibited from talking during breakfast, so the servers slammed food on our metal trays, and then we went to sit and gulp down our food.

After breakfast, we went to our room and discovered all our beds torn apart and on the floor. One of the drill instructors followed us into the room and explained that if he couldn't bounce a quarter off the bed, it wasn't done correctly, and thus gave us our first class of the day. He instructed all the troops on how to put a bed together. All we needed to do was pull the hell out of the sheets and top blanket, then tuck it hard under the mattress. After the room was perfect, the drill instructor tossed a quarter on the bed, and the quarter bounced. He looked at us all and said that was what he would expect tomorrow. We made our beds, and then we headed out in company formation. We were greeted by a group and informed about taking a seat. We were all informed of why we were in training. And that we would be learning how to handle and provide orders. While attending this Academy, we were to have a ten-minute break every hour on the hour.

After the third class, it was time for lunch. We were doubled-timed to the mess hall, taking turns leading the cadence counting and platoon leader from one location to another. We had to learn; this cadence of counting and leading was good. After lunch, we spent double the time back in the classroom area.

Some of our training was out in the field or on the ranges. When we started on a map and a compass course, that was easy for me. Most of our training was to teach us how to take control, take orders, and give orders.

Hackett, another newly made friend, and I went out on a pass one Saturday afternoon. There was a carnival in town, and we wanted to go and have a little enjoyment. Going to the carnival would make a good break from classes. Hackett and I went to the carnival and lost all our paychecks; maybe it was our fault to gamble on the mouse game. I'll let you know I have never played that game again; I've learned my lesson. Hackett and I left the carnival area and bought a few beers with our last few bucks.

A military bus came by the fairgrounds and took us back to the base. Hackett and I returned to our barracks, took our school information to the day room, and studied between pool games.

Come Monday morning back to classroom work. I couldn't wait for this school to be done and over with. Due to personal reasons, I dropped out of the Academy with one week left; I will not discuss it. I took the military bus back to Friedberg, and returning to my daily duties felt good. I had lost my acting Sergeant stripes. The first sergeant was upset at me and stuck me on KP for a week.

Chapter Twenty-Seven

Koplin Guard

Every once in a while, the company had to pull Guard Duty at an ammo dump, and my best guess was Koplin Guard. Koplin is where the Brigade had much of its ammo in underground bunkers. There were not too many soldiers who enjoyed or liked this duty. We arrived in Koplin for a few days.

Once we arrived at the ammo dump, we had to pass through two well-guarded gates. We went to the bunkhouse to settle down. If you have ever seen the TV show *Hogan's Heroes*, our bunkhouse was like the ones you see on that show. We had to bring our sleeping bags since our beds had no sheets. This guard duty had to be the worst in Germany; even a three-day alert was better than Koplin.

We were on duty for four hours and off for four hours around the clock for a week. There were two fences surrounding the entire perimeter, inside and out. Our job was to patrol between the two fences. At some point, the two fences were only about eight feet apart, and in other areas, they could be as far as one hundred feet apart, with sections passing through wooded areas and fields. Jones, one of the guys who came with me to Berchtesgaden, was on the same watch. I think he was a bit loony at times. While he and I walked the perimeter in different locations, I heard a gunshot, which brought some of the leaders from the guard station running to investigate. I ran toward the gunshot to find out what in hell was happening. Several people were investigating when I arrived at the scene. It was getting dusk, and daylight was fading. What had happened was that Jones saw something move and heard a lot of noise. Jones could not comprehend what was happening even after he yelled, "Halt and identify yourself!" He repeated it twice and then added, "I will shoot you if you do not identify yourself!" He followed the protocol as we were instructed.

We discovered he was a good shot; he had killed an owl that swooped down to attack a rabbit. The rabbit got away, but the owl didn't. Jones was off guard duty for the remainder of the week, which was lucky for him.

On the following day, during one of my watches. I had to walk along the outer fence at the far end of the perimeter. While walking this section at the ammo dump, I could see a group of small gardens where locals planted summer plots. Most of those gardens had small sheds to store gardening tools, and some were large enough to hold other items like chairs and charcoal grills.

This one afternoon, while walking out in that area, I saw a couple of young girls sunbathing nude. I was stunned and didn't go far from my vision of the girls. I stopped for a while and just looked; this was when I should have had my camera handy. We were not able to bring a camera to this highly secure area. I made another walk around and came right back to this area. This time, I noticed something wrong with the fence. It looked like someone had grabbed the bottom of the fence on our side and lifted the barrier, creating a crawl space to get on the other side.

On my next watch, I quickly returned to the area I was in earlier. It was late and dark, and the girls were gone by then. Hopefully, the next day, the girls would return to sunbathe. The next day, while I was out on the outer perimeter, I saw some people working in their gardens. I did see the two girls working in their garden. I think they saw me near the fence. I spotted them looking my way, and when they saw me this time, they waved. I waved back.

After gardening, they removed their chairs from the little shed. My eyes were on them. They slowly took off their clothes except for their underwear. They noticed I was watching and waved at me again. I returned the hand wave. I also noticed the fence still needed repair, and as a guard, it was my responsibility to report the hole. One of the girls came to the fence and asked if I'd be interested in crawling under it. As tempting as the invitation was, I didn't crawl under the fence. Damn, she had nice, perky breasts, with her nipples pointing toward me.

This girl told me she often came to the garden to meet some of the men in hopes of getting a date for later, after the troops returned to their barracks. She gave me her address, and I took it. She pressed her breasts against the fence and asked if I liked them. She spoke some broken English, so I could not understand what she was saying. I just looked at her and returned a wide, friendly smile for an answer.

When I returned to the guard shack, I was going to report the hole in the fence, but I thought I'd wait until just before we left to return to Friedberg. I returned to the Guard shack, and dinner, which had arrived from Friedberg, was waiting. The food sucked because it was created hours earlier; some food was cold and mushy.

The last day of Koplin duty was here, and we were glad to be leaving; this duty was harsh on anybody. Our reliefs arrived, and we packed up our belongings and headed back to our barracks in Friedberg. When we returned, I went to the orderly room to request a three-day pass. Smith and I planned another trip to Amsterdam. We'd be leaving right after retreat on Friday; this would be a four-hour train ride.

Chapter Twenty-Eight
Weekend In Amsterdam

Friday afternoon, Sergeant Smith and I packed up to leave right after the last company formation. We had our bags, so we took a cab to the Bahnhof in town. We had to stop and transfer in Frankfort; we were held over for about an hour, giving us enough time for a beer. Back at the platform, we saw our train arriving. As people were getting off, we hopped on and found an empty compartment, so we entered and placed our bags on the overhead racks. Two Russian girls entered our chamber and sat down. We introduced ourselves, and they did the same. They also were headed to The Netherlands. Once the train left, the conductor came in to check out tickets, and all was well.

Within a few minutes after, we left the station. The Russian girls opened their bags, took bottles of Cognac from them, and placed them under and between the seats. It was going to be a five-hour train ride to Amsterdam. At this time, Sergeant Smith and I went to the dining car to get something to drink. We took the beers to our compartment. We didn't trust those Russians, especially after seeing them hide their Cognac. When it came time to cross into The Netherlands, the border police entered the train. When they arrived in our compartment, they checked our passes and ID. The police wanted Sergeant Smith and me to open our bags for inspection. The police never asked to check the girls' bags or even searched the compartment. I guess girls are to be trusted, and men can't be.

Once we arrived in Amsterdam, we took a cab to Canal Street to a small Gasthaus for a couple of bucks a night. We had a place to stay on Canal Street called Silver Dollar. Canal Street is where many girls sell themselves for a quick lay. All we had to do was walk down the street and do some window shopping. The hookers would sit before a window and display their hot bodies. In the daytime, they would sit with only their bra and panties. Later in the evening, they sometimes would take off their bras to drum up more business as there was more merchandise to see. I was just a bystander as I remember what happened to me the last and only time I got laid. I wasn't taking any chances on getting VD again. That almost cost me my life, as you may recall.

We each rented a bed in a large room with about a dozen beds; I guess we rented a bed just for a place to sleep. Oh well, it's no worse than the barracks. We met Steve, who also was in our company. Every time I went to Amsterdam, I would meet someone from the company. I'd visited Amsterdam at least twice a year for the time I was in Germany for three years.

Sergeant Smith, Steve, and I spent a few hours at the Gasthaus (Silver Dollar) bar where we stayed. When making plans for the next day, I was the only one who wanted to go to Zandvoort, which has a significant and beautiful beach. It is also a clothing-optional beach. There are miles of beaches and many enjoyable views for your eyes.

The next day, the three of us went to a local restaurant for lunch, and from there, I went on my own. We were warned not to travel alone for safety reasons. As a young man, I didn't want to miss the opportunity to be on a nude beach on the North Sea. I loved The Netherlands. This country is lovely, and the people seem to be very friendly.

Zandvoort is where I had to travel to get to the nude beaches; it was about 45 minutes by train. The station wasn't too far away from the Silver Dollar. I walked to the station and purchased a round-trip ticket. It cost me about twenty Guilders for the ticket. I sat in the dining car to consume some good Holland beer. I'm a slow drinker; drinking two beers will take about 40 minutes. I was right; it took me the whole trip to drink the two beers.

After leaving the train station, I checked the schedule for the return trips to Amsterdam. Trains leave every hour to Amsterdam, and this is what I liked about living in the European Community: you don't need to own a car. Trains were my daily mode of travel through central Europe; in any large city, we had the underground and trolleys to get around. Stepping out at the train station felt good; I could smell the fresh sea air from the North Sea; it reminded me of the beaches in Maine.

I headed toward the sandy beaches; this end of the beach was where most of the working girls hung around to get tan all over. There were no tan lines for these girls. These working women looked fine lying on the beach in front of me on a blanket in the nude. At first, I couldn't stop looking at the naked bodies; I stopped and removed my shoes, socks, shirt, and pants. I did keep my boxer shorts on. I did have a bath towel, which I laid on the hot white sand; I laid on the towel and enjoyed the fantastic views.

I felt so refreshed lying on the beach; being from the state of Maine, I was used to sandy beaches. Life was relaxing, and I enjoyed a day away from work after about an hour of lying in the sun. I picked myself up from the ground, put on my pants, and carried the rest of my clothes under my arm. I walked down the beach until I arrived at a boardwalk. I then located an outside cafe and sat. The waitress came to the table to take my order; of course, I ordered beer for a drink, and I also ordered a loaded hamburger. While looking around, I spotted two beautiful girls walking by, and I winked at them. They saw me, came to the table, and asked if they could sit there. So, I bought them a drink, and we talked for a while, finding out they were from Amsterdam and were not working girls. They both had jobs working at a hotel, and they had a day off. We talked for a long while, and when we noticed the time, it was getting late. I told the girls I had to leave as I had to meet my roommates later. We said our goodbyes and shook hands, and I got warm hugs from the girls; that was the last time I ever saw these girls. I went to the train station and waited for the next train.

I was walking toward the train station. It took me about fifteen minutes to get there. I checked out the schedule on the wall post, and it showed that the train should come in about 20 minutes, just enough time for another quick beer. I was sitting at a sidewalk cafe with my shirt off and enjoying an ice-cold beer. I noticed many girls checking me out as they walked by. A few of the girls walking by would look at me, smile, and say hi to me as they passed. I couldn't resist but to return the smile and say hi. Finally, one girl stopped to talk to me and asked if she could sit with me. I stood up and moved a chair, and we sat down. I offered to purchase her a beer, and she accepted the offer. She drank half her beer, and I told her I had to catch a train back to Amsterdam. I got up, said goodbye to the girl but never got her name, and returned to the station. At times, I believe girls are more aggressive than men.

I arrived back just in time to catch the train. I sat in an open car with some seats near a window. I love looking out from the train windows as the countryside is so beautiful and there is much to see. I arrived in Amsterdam on schedule, then headed out to meet the others at the Silver Dollar bar. Sure enough, they were there waiting for me so we could get some nightlife started. Disco was prominent in the sixties, and that's where we headed from outside. We didn't have to go too far to locate a nightclub. There was a small cover charge of one Guilder to get into the club.

Once inside, we found a table to sit down at. No sooner had we sat down than the waitress was there to get our orders, and we ordered a pitcher of beer with three glasses. It wasn't long before I got the nerve to ask strangers to dance with me. I'm a sucker for blondes with blue eyes, and being in The Netherlands, I was in the perfect place. The first girl I asked to dance with turned me down, so I went to a table where a group of girls sat, and they were all blondes. The first girl I asked to dance with at that table accepted my offer. We went to the dance floor, which wasn't more significant than a twelve-foot square area. We started to dance on the crowded dance floor, which was overcrowded, making it impossible not to touch each other—dancing this close together and our bodies touching and rubbing together. This girl, I didn't get her name, didn't have a bra on, and I felt great with her breasts flat on my chest. I could feel her hard nipples pressing against me, and I was more than optimistic she could feel my throbbing manhood against her leg.

After a few dances, I noticed Sergeant Smith was also on the dance floor. The music was loud, and the place was full of smoke from people smoking. Smoking didn't bother me currently because I had picked up smoking since being in the Army. After a few more dances, the band stopped for a break. Everybody went to their seats, and some people even left the club. We finished a third pitcher of beer and then left the club ourselves. We walked down Canal Street, where window shopping was in full swing. I wasn't over my fear of catching VD from any of the girls. Sergeant Smith did some window shopping until he saw someone hot-looking, sexy girl he wanted to have sex with. I sat along the canal on a bench and watched all the men looking to get laid.

After Sergeant Smith got laid and joined me back on the sidewalk, we continued along the canal until we arrived at our hotel. We went into the building and to the room we shared with others. We took a few minutes to discuss what we'd be doing the next day, and there was a brewery not far from Canal Street. The next day, we took some time to walk through the red-light district and enjoy a day of sightseeing on foot.

We left the hotel just before noon and walked to the city center toward the Train Station. We passed many storefronts with many different wares for sale. There were many sex novelties, shops, restaurants, clubs, and all sorts of things you'd have to see to believe. We arrived at the Heineken Brewery, and there was already a line outside the building waiting for the next tour. It wasn't long before our group entered the next tour. The time was fascinating and very informative. After the tour, we went to a room where we could sample their beer and a sample of different types of cheese.

At the table where I was sitting, I met a girl from the States. We talked to each other, and she told me where she lived. I was baffled when she told me she was on a European tour with her parents. She told me her name was Amy, and she was from Fairfield, the next town from where I lived in Maine. This town borders my city, and she lived only 2 miles from my home. We arranged to meet later that evening at a local nightclub, and from there, we departed from each other's company. Smith and I left the brewery and headed to the city center for more sightseeing.

At the city center was a statue where many people would sit and enjoy the scenery, the passing trolleys, walking by or riding a bicycle, parents pushing a baby buggy, and other exciting sites. There were many outside cafes, and we sat at one of them. We drank some more beer while passing the time away and enjoying our little time on our leave. We spent about two hours sipping beer and trying to attract some ladies from nearby tables to join us. We talked to a few passing ladies but couldn't convince anyone to join us at the table.

Time passed, and I returned to the hotel to clean up before my date. I left Sergeant Smith as he had other plans when he found out I had a date. We arrived on Canal Street, where the famous window shopping was happening, our hotel's street. We entered the hotel through the front lobby, and the barmaid saw us enter and motioned us to come to the bar. As soon as we reached the bar, she poured us a drink. I didn't want to have any more to drink. I just wanted to get cleaned up as it was getting late and close to the time for my date. I gulped the drink down and placed two Guilder pieces on the bar for a tip, and I left; I thanked the barmaid.

Arriving at the club, I stood outside as this was how we said we would meet. I must have waited about fifteen minutes before Amy showed up. She was a beauty neatly dressed for the occasion. We went to the nightclub, which was a disco club. After I paid the cover charge to get into the club, just about every club had a cover charge, and then we were escorted to a table for two. We ordered, and within a few minutes, our drinks arrived. I had a beer, and Amy had a rum and coke.

At first, we didn't hit the dance floor, but we sat down and talked for a while to get to know each other. We found out we knew some of the same people from back home. Amy had just graduated from high school, and this trip was a gift from her parents. After a while, we hit the dance floor; disco music was it. We danced the bump. We bumped, pushed, and pulled on each other. We finally got to have a slow dance. Like any young person, there is nothing like getting on a dance floor with bodies touching and feeling each other up with a free hand. Amy had a perfect build for her size and age; she was barely nineteen, and I was twenty. We were almost neighbors back home about three thousand miles away from Amsterdam.

We found a little corner where we went so we could caress and kiss each other; it was like this night was for us to be together. She had her hands all over me, and I had my hands all over her while we were both French kissing. She could tell that I was hard. She had small breasts and didn't mind when I brushed my hands over them. She told me which hotel she stayed at; her parents had one room, and she had a room. Amy asked if I would like to go to her room.

We arrived at her hotel; at first, I wasn't allowed to enter the hotel because I didn't have a jacket. Amy let the doorman know she was a guest at the hotel and that I needed a dress jacket. The doorman retrieved a coat for me to wear to get into the hotel, a little class. Amy and I entered the elevator; as soon as the doors closed, we locked lips and were getting heavy making out. The elevator came to a stop, and the doors opened, and that ended our date. Her dad was at the elevator door waiting for Amy to return; he looked furious. She stepped out, and

I went to the lobby floor, dropped my jacket off, and headed out of the hotel.

Leaving the hotel, I went to a trolley stop to check how to return to Canal Street. Sure enough, there was a trolley that would take me back to Canal Street. When I arrived at the hotel room, Sergeant Smith was already in bed but not asleep. He told me he had packed his bag and was ready to leave in the morning. Knowing this, I got my bag ready for the trip back to Frankfurt.

We were ready to return to Germany the following day after breakfast. At breakfast, Sergeant Smith asked how my night with Amy had gone. After spending about half an hour telling him how my night went, we couldn't stop laughing. We finally called it a day and went to bed. In the morning, we cleaned up and ensured we didn't leave anything behind. We went to the lobby with our bags, checked out, and then walked to the train station. Our train ride back to Frankfurt went without interruption.

Chapter Twenty-Nine

NATO Exercise

I woke up at Monday's first call and finished my morning cleaning duties. Sergeant Downs came to the room to talk with me. He and I went to the day room, where he told me there would be a NATO exercise in a couple of days. The track drivers and the track commander were the only members of our platoon participating in this exercise. We would be training with the British Army. The unit we were to work with was not mechanized and would use our vehicles, drivers, and track commanders. After explaining what would occur, I realized this sounded like a great time to work with the British Army. Company formation sounded, and we all fell out to the company formation. After the headcount, some individuals returned to the barracks, and the rest visited the mess hall.

Work call rang, and on this day, the drivers were to meet at the motor pool for instruction on what we would be doing while training with the British. Once the information was given, we cleaned the track. I moved everything off the track that I was allowed to. I cleaned the track thoroughly and even added a little paint where needed. While working on the track, Sergeant Bundy came to me and asked if I'd be interested in attending an eight-week course at a radio school in Lenggries.

Later that evening, a group of us went to the club, where there was live entertainment. Layton, Victor, Huff, and I arrived early to get a good seat. The club had a lit glass floor. As I entered the club, I looked to the right and saw the slot machines. I wanted to play, but my friends were more important, so I joined them at a table. That night, the performers were a group of girls only; they were singers, and none played any instruments. An instrumental group of local townspeople provided the music. I didn't stay at the EM club long since I had a demanding workday ahead. I left the club, went to the barracks, and called it a night.

Morning came, and I had to prepare my track for NATO training with the British. Sergeant Downs and I were in the motor pool, doing a quick checklist inspection to ensure we had everything we needed for the railhead.

It was time to head to the railhead for another field problem. This one, however, was different from all the others I had participated in. Once at the railhead, we waited to board the track on the flatbed railcar. Sergeant Downs guided me along the flatbed cars to the one we would tie down on. It was not my first time doing this, but Sergeant Downs and I had done it in record time. The passenger train had already attached to the flatbed cars. We walked down the tracks until we reached the train car assigned to us, boarded the train, and looked for a compartment that wasn't full.

The trip went by quickly for me as I slept most of the trip. I had a lot on my mind; this NATO exercise and then the radio school were a lot to take in a short time. When I returned, I'd have to re-adjust myself in our company's communication department. Of course, I would also want to try to transfer to Division Headquarters to be with my twin brother, Gil. I finally dozed off; before I knew it, it was dinner time. There was a dining car on this train, and we were allowed to get something to eat.

We arrived at the destination the following day, quickly got our vehicles off the flatbed cars, and headed to the training area where the British were waiting for us. While we drove our vehicles through the small villages, the townspeople would line the streets. Little children would do the same, but the little children would have their little hands stretched out toward us, asking for handouts.

Arriving at the British training area, we met some British military officials. We went to their motor pool, where we parked our vehicles for the night. Once I had the track secured and locked, we marched to a location where we were seated, and this is where we met the British we were to be training with. After the presentation, we were dismissed and brought to the barracks where we would stay. We would be on post at night. There would be some nights on which we would be on overnight training.

We attended a few classes to get information on what was to take place while training. After the classes, we went to the barracks to which we were assigned and settled in by unpacking our gear. Some British troops called us to go out for a drink at one of the clubs on the base. The British knew how to put away their Whiskey. On this trip, I'd try to stay to a two-beer-a-night limit. These British troops would not let us buy our drinks; they insisted they pay, and there is nothing wrong with that.

Bright and early the following morning, we were in the mess hall in no time to have breakfast. After breakfast, we met the British we would train with. We would leave within the hour, and Sergeant Downs and I headed to the motor pool. Once at the motor pool, we got the track ready for our training guests. We secured all equipment to the track so as not to get in the way of the troops. I'm sure the troops wanted to stick their heads out of the open hatch. I didn't need to top off as I didn't even use ten gallons of fuel. The fuel tank could hold 180 gallons of fuel.

I started the track and dropped the rear ramp to allow the training personnel to get on board. Besides, Sargent Downs and I were 6 British with us: their squad leader and five-foot soldiers. I accelerated on the gas, raised the rear ramp, locked it in place, and went off. I had a radio communication with the track commander on my headgear. Sergeant Downs allowed the British squad leader to command the track this time. I drove, following the rest of the tracks and tanks. Once we arrived at a large open field, we spread out, and each track was assigned to follow a tank. I'd follow the tank when the tank would stop, and I would stop if the track commander ordered me to drop the ramp. I knew the troops would come out in an assault line, along with three other teams. Such a move would mean about twenty-four troopers running in a line toward their objective. We did this several times during the day for practice and training purposes.

Every hour, we'd form a wagon wheel in a circle for a tea break for about 10 minutes and then back to training. We ran more training for a few hours; it was dinner time. The mess truck came with our dinner, and the food was okay for being in the field. It took us about an hour for dinner and then back to the training with the British. That night, we had to operate without lights, and no smoking was allowed as it would give our position away.

For the rest of the night, I stayed in my tracks. The British had to dig in and dig two men's foxholes to accommodate them for the night. They also had to do recon missions; Sergeant Downs and I slept inside the track as the British troops continued to do their training.

The morning was upon us, and we had to make a quick move; with the track running, I lowered the back ramp, the troops entered, and off we went. I just listened to my track commander and followed his orders. Before breakfast, we did a few military maneuvers; the mess truck wasn't too far away. When we arrived near the mess area, we circled the mess truck. We enjoyed breakfast before returning to the company barracks. Once we were back on base, the British left the motor pool, and we drivers and track commanders were left behind, so we cleaned out the track. After cleaning the track, I took it to the wash racks to remove all the dirt and mud, then went to top it off with fuel. Once I finished cleaning up the track, Sergeant Downs and I went to the barracks. Arriving at the barracks and being instructed to report to a particular building, the troops were getting more instructions for our next training assignment. The troops were given the night off, and training would continue in the morning.

I made friends with some British Troops; some of us got together and went off the post to a local bar. We were not to wear military clothing while on a pass to go into town. We did plenty of drinking and also got involved in some foosball playing. Playing foosball against some German troops was almost impossible to beat; they were good at it.

There was a small dance floor at this bar, which I used. I had a few dances with a couple of local girls. Many German girls loved to meet us Americans; in some cases, it was a way for some girls to get to the States. Some troops would make friends, marry the German girls, and take them stateside when they rotated to the States.

After a couple of hours of drinking and enjoying time with my newly made friends, I returned to the base for the night and needed rest before the next training day. When I arrived at the barracks, some guys were getting ready for the next day. I took a little time to write a couple of letters to my family back home, and I also wrote to Gail of Bolton, England, telling her about my time training with the NATO troops.

After the next few days of training with the NATO Forces, our unit was making plans to return to Friedberg to be with the rest of our home teams. I have decided to attend radio school in Lenggries. I went to see Sergeant Downs and told him I would be interested in attending radio school when we returned. Returning to school would mean I would have less than a week to prepare for my new radio communication adventure.

After our NATO training, we packed our belongings and headed home, never to see these newly made friends again. As always, we traveled on an overnight train ride back to Friedberg. The train ride back was an excellent time to rest and sleep. Waking up as we arrived at the train yard in Friedberg, Sergeant Downs and I hurried out to the flatbed cars where our track was. We took down the tie-down equipment in no time and waited our turn to drive off the flatbed cars.

Driving off the flatbed cars and straight to our motor pool, I returned to the barracks to unpack my gear.

I met with Sergeant Bundy to talk about the radio school; he told me he anticipated my decision and had already made my application. Talking to Sergeant Bundy about my chances of getting transferred to Division Headquarters, he told me he would disapprove of my request. In other words, I had no choice but to attend school. I had until Saturday before I left for Lenggries, so I had better get my plans made.

I had the rest of the day off to prepare for the all-day trip to Lenggries. I called Gil and told him I was visiting Frankfort to visit with him and that we could do something together. He said he was still at work, so I would have to go to his office to see him and also visit with his office crew.

I walked out of the back gate and to the Bahnhof, only waiting a few minutes for the train. A few minutes later, I arrived at the City Center train station, where I took the subway and then a bus to get to his place of work at headquarters.

I checked in at the front gate and went to Gil's office, where he worked; I met his boss in the hall and greeted him with a salute. He returned the salute. I entered Gil's office, and the Colonel arrived within a few minutes. I got ready to salute him when he stopped me and said I didn't have to compliment him every time I saw him in the building; once in the building is enough, he told me. He again asked me when I was coming to headquarters to work for him; I told him I was trying.

After Gil finished his work, we headed to the open mess hall for dinner. I met a couple of his friends, and they sat with us. Gil and I were planning what we should do for the evening because I would attend radio school for two months. Gil and I decided to stay at the base that night, and we'd go to the club as there would be live entertainment. Some group from England was going to perform for the troops. When the club had live entertainment, the club got crowded, so we had to get there early. We left the mess hall and went to Gil's room so he could get cleaned up and head to the club.

Chapter-Thirty
Radio School

After dropping out of NCO Academy, the first sergeant gave me all sorts of unpleasant details. My job was becoming more stressful, and I needed a way to leave the company. I requested a spot at radio school as an escape. I placed the request for the communications school in Lenggries, located at the foot of the Alps. My application was accepted, and I was off to school again.

Within a few days, before I had to be at radio school, I made plans and arrangements for the trip to Lenggries. Before leaving, I entered the orderly room to pick up my travel orders and travel tickets.

The train ride to Lenggries took just over 6 hours. When I arrived at the Lenggries Bahnhof, a military jeep was waiting to take me to the base. We hopped into the jeep, and within minutes, we were at the Kaserne.

Once at the Kaserne, I reported to the school's orderly room. I registered as a student for the radio school and was then shown to a room I would call home for the next eight weeks.

The room must have had at least 20 beds. I picked a bunk at random, choosing the one at the far end of the room on the right side. I had the rest of the day to settle in, and my instruction was to report to a particular classroom the following day.

I was unpacking my duffel bag, putting my clothes in a wall locker and my stuff in a footlocker. As I was doing this, some other troops entered and chose bunks to settle in like I was. Within a couple of hours, the room was occupied entirely by students. I met a few of the guys that day. It was time for dinner, and we headed to the mess hall to fill our stomachs. While at the dinner table with my newly made friends, we exchanged information about ourselves and got to know each other better as we were to be neighbors for the next eight weeks. After dinner, a few of us went out looking around the base for the EM club to have drinks. After asking someone for directions to the club, we walked there in a few minutes.

This club was smaller than the one in Friedberg but had all the same amenities. We sat at an empty table, and within a few minutes, we had beers. One of the guys at the table, Smitty, became a friend while I was at the radio school. We agreed that if the instructor would pair people together at any time while in classes, we would be a team. We had a few beers, but not enough to get us drunk. I learned my lesson from drinking too much; I have learned when to stop and not to get too drunk. We may have stayed at the club for a couple of hours, then returned to the barracks to call it a night; we had to get up at 0600 hours for the first call.

After breakfast, we marched to the classroom for our introduction to the course. This training was much better than any other training I have had since joining the Army. After our first day of classroom work, we were allowed to do what we wanted while in Southern Bavaria near the Austrian border, about twelve miles away.

That evening, Smitty and I went to the USO club on post. We learned that we could take day trips on the weekends sponsored by the USO. We looked at the schedules to see what we could plan for the weekend. We were also allowed to sign out on passes while at school. One exciting place to visit and check out was in Bad Tolz, about ten miles away. We'd have to travel by bus or hire a cab to get to Bad Tolz.

After the next day of classes, Smitty and I signed out for a pass and went to town to find a good German restaurant and food. The food at the Kaserne mess hall was food from an American menu. I love the Wienerschnitzel with potato salad, green vegetables, and a cold beer. We found this quaint little Gasthaus not far from the Kaserne. After looking at the menu outside the door entrance, we decided to go in for dinner. The food was excellent, and we enjoyed our little time there, enjoying our food and listening to German music.

After dinner, we walked around the little village of Lenggries. The sites were just beautiful and settled at the base of the Alps. Undoubtedly, we would find our way to the Brauneck Gipfelhaus on top of nearby Brauneck Mountain. There were two ways to get there: one was by cable, and the other was to hike up the mountain on well-marked trails. We were going to hike and ride at different times. We returned to the Kaserne, but before we went to the barracks, we stopped by the USO club, which was still open. We again checked some tourist flyers to see what we could do in the coming days. We observed on the following weekend that there was a tour to a southern Bavarian Castle, Neuschwanstein Castle, which was a free tour, so Smitty and I signed up for next Sunday.

Classes were five days a week from 0800 hours through 1500 hours. We were given homework on the first day of school. This instructor told us that all our tests would be open books. We were not to have any notebooks except our textbook on our desks while taking a test. He did tell us that it was up to us if we wanted to place notes in the textbook, which would be allowed on our desks for the tests. We could not fail any of his tests with the open-book exams. All this radio stuff was new, and I had to learn quickly.

After the third day of class, Smitty and I signed out to go into the villages. This time, we'd head out to Bad Tolz to find out how to get up Brauneck Mountain. Once, we arrived in Bad Tolz on the local bus, which stopped us near the Bahnhof. We entered the Bahnhof as we knew there was always an information booth where someone could answer questions about the area. The bus conductor directed us toward the cable cars that would take people up Brauneck Mountain. The trip up the mountain was one DM for a round trip. We purchased a round-trip ticket and headed up the cable for new adventures.

Once up the mountain, there were a few buildings, one being a Gasthaus, where we would have a couple of beers after walking around the mountain paths to get some great views of the surrounding area, more mountains, and many more valleys. I didn't have a camera, and I wished I did; you don't see sites like this daily. Maybe someday I will return to this beautiful area. We did have enough time for a couple of beers at the Gasthaus before heading back to the cable to get back into Bad Tolz.

Back at the Kaserne, Smitty and I went to the barracks to review what we learned today in class. Reading the radio schematic was worse than the map reading classes I took at the NCO Academy. The radio schematics took much studying, and a short time later, the light bulb over my head went off, and the class improved.

The lights went off, and we all went to bed. It was quiet, and everyone quickly fell asleep. A soldier across the room woke me up, and soon, the other soldiers were stirred, too. We all laughed about it later. Someone across the room from me was having a dream. He dreamed he was home with his wife and making love while still sleeping. This soldier exited, got into the bed next to his, and started climbing on another guy, waking him up. Funny, we laughed for days about it. I guess you can never tell what a person can do when sleepwalking.

With our trip to Neuschwanstein Castle just a few days away, Smitty and I wanted to save a few bucks, knowing we'd have to pay for our meals. We decided to go to the local club on base. On the way from the barracks to the club was a training area where the Green Berets trained German Sheppard dogs as attack dogs. We'd sometimes stop to watch some of the dogs in action. The Green Berets always thought they were better than we were. That night at the club, one of the troopers in school with us got into a scuffle with a green-beret soldier. It was primarily just words, and team members separated them from both sides. After a while, I had to go to the bathroom. The guy who started the scuffle was in the bathroom. He spotted someone's green beret, threw it in the trough, and urinated on it. I left because I wanted nothing to do with the Green Berets. I wasn't the type of person who looked for trouble. I went to see Smitty and told him what had happened in the men's room; he and I left the club as we didn't want to get involved with the results of this incident. There were soldiers from all over Germany for some schooling and some training.

The class was over at 1500 hours on Friday. The troops went back to the barracks, and most of them were to make plans for the weekend. Some troops not stationed too far away would take a bus or train back to their home Base. I don't remember where in Germany Smitty was stationed; he and I had made plans to take that trip to the Castle.

After dinner, we changed into civvies and walked to the USO, hoping to meet some local girls. It was still early, so we might have a chance to meet someone to spend some time with. We noticed a few girls sitting at a table as we entered. Smitty and I parted ways to see if we could encounter some hot babe. I approached a table where a girl was there by herself. I asked if I could sit with her, and she motioned me to the chair beside her. I found out she was here alone, and her father was in the military, and she wanted to meet someone who was an American.

We talked and got to know each other within a few minutes. I asked the young lady her name and if she wanted a soft drink, and she accepted. She told me her name was June. I asked June if she wanted anything to drink, and she said yes. I handed her the soft drink when I returned to the table. We talked some more; I found out her father was a Major on temporary duty as an instructor at one of the schools at the Kaserne. June was a senior in high school. She was eighteen, which made me two years older than she was. Army brats were sometimes rebellious against their parents, and she didn't like moving around every two to three years. June was a very pretty-looking girl.

It wasn't long before the music started for the Friday night dance. We didn't dance right off as we were still getting information about each other to understand better who we were to each other. Looking around the room, I noticed Smitty also found someone and was talking to a girl. Being only twenty years old and being with a girl who understood everything we discussed was relaxing. I asked June for a dance, and she accepted. We danced to disco music. We had a great time dancing, and after a few songs, we returned to the table and talked more. June was from the Atlanta, GA, area; that was her family's hometown.

The music shifted to a slower tempo, and I asked June if she wanted to dance slowly with me. She agreed, and we headed to the dance floor we went. We started off dancing slowly and not too close to each other, as I didn't want June to feel I was pushing myself onto her. As the music played and we danced, June pulled herself closer to me as our bodies touched. Her body felt terrific against mine, and I was sure she could feel my manhood against her leg. She wrapped her arms around me, and we just danced in the heat of our bodies, making friction rubbing together.

After two slow dances, we returned to sit at our table; June excused herself as she had to go to the ladies' room. That gave me time to let Smitty know we were alone for the rest of the night. As I arrived back at the table, I could see June coming back to the table. Before she sat down, she moved her chair closer to mine. Once seated, she grabbed my hand and just wanted to hold me by the hand. We started to talk more and found out more about each other. June told me it was tough to find a male friend because her father was an officer constantly moving from place to place.

June even got close to me; at this time, she put her arm around me, closed in on my lips, and planted a small kiss on me. We got up for another dance when a slow song came up. We danced slowly and close together this time; she smelled like a fresh flower. She excited me again, and I know she enjoyed doing this to me. June was grinding into me, and I enjoyed it as much as she did. I felt she wasn't a virgin the way she was playing me. We locked lips on the dance floor; after a few minutes, June asked if I wanted to leave the building with her. How could I refuse her invitation? We finished the dance and left the USO club, and I motioned to Smitty as I went, giving him the peace sign.

June headed to the parking lot. On the way, she told me she had her father's car, and we had to be careful not to mess it up or disturb the inside. We got into the car and drove off; we hadn't gone far when June pulled into a parking lot near a small stream/river that flowed through the village. When June stopped the car, she opened her door, looked at me, and said, Let us walk down by the river. It was dark then, and a few lights in the parking lot put out enough light so we could see where we were walking. Once we got to the riverbank, there were some benches, and we sat at one. We sat close together and got back into the kissing and heavy petting. We got into some petting and feeling each other, which felt great. We also got to talk a lot more; we exchanged our addresses to write to each other. We were there for about a half hour and decided to leave. Her father gave her a curfew to follow.

On the way back to the barracks, she asked if we could see each other again soon. I told June I had a few weeks before returning to Friedberg. I let her know I would love to meet her again. We made plans to meet again next Friday at the club. Arriving back at the Kaserne, we kissed briefly and then parted ways.

As I headed toward the building, June drove away. I entered the barracks, and Smitty was already back in his bunk. He came over, and we chatted for a little while. From our short talk, it seems I was luckier than he was. Lights out and to bed till the first call, a well-needed night's sleep on the way.

Smitty and I had planned to go to Bad Tolz and hike up Brauneck Mountain as it was Saturday, and we had all day to do this climb; believe me, it would take all day. We planned to hike up and take the cable back to town. After getting cleaned for the day and cleaning up around my sleeping area, Smitty and I went to have a healthy breakfast before leaving for our hike up the Alps.

Getting off the bus in Bad Tolz, we walked toward the cable car station. That is where the trail started on the way to the foot of the mountain, about a mile away. I noticed a couple of outside cafes, which were places where they also sold beer. One thing I learned to do for the short time I had been in the Army was beer drinking. We stopped at the first Gasthaus for only one beer. It was a warm day, and we had a long hike ahead. Shortly after getting to the Gasthaus, we'd finished the beer and headed on the trail that led us up the mountain. This road was a dirt road and very winding. There was one area where we climbed a rough site to cut some winding trails. We would have been better off staying on the path, but we had to learn the hard way.

Walking on the trail, we passed a few houses where people lived. I don't know how people can live in areas like this. It was the Alps, and the winters here are terrible. We also came upon a few small streams which flowed down the mountain. We knew we were going the correct way as the trail was marked.

Once at the top of Brauneck Mountain, we walked by the cable terminal and headed toward the Gasthaus, a few hundred feet away. Once we entered the place, we were welcomed and escorted to a table where we sat and ordered a beer. The beer was well-deserved after that long walk up the Alps. We also had some excellent German food to eat. We knew the last cable run down the mountain was at 1800 hours. After we had eaten and put down a couple of beers, we left the Gasthaus and walked one of the trails, and there were many of them. All the trails are well-marked so as not to get lost.

We were heading back to the cable terminal to catch the last cable car back down to the village of Bad Tolz. Oh shit, we missed the last cable car for the day. We must have missed it by just a few minutes because we could see it traveling down on the cable. Smitty and I looked at each other in disbelief because we had missed the cable car and planned to catch the bus to Neuschwanstein Castle in the morning. We turned back and headed back to the Gasthaus, and I asked the waitress if she knew when the cable started back down the mountain in the morning. She told me the first cable car leaves at 0600 hours to Bad Tolz.

I went to the bar and asked the innkeeper how much it would cost to stay the night; she replied, Twenty DM for both of us. I showed the Inn Keeper a 1964 Kennedy fifty-cent piece and asked her what it was worth. She told me she'd take the half dollar to take care of the room for the night. Kennedy was a well-liked person back then.

The bus journey to the Castle departs at 1000 hours from the Service club. Catching the cable car at 0600 would give us plenty of time to get back to the barracks, clean up, and make the bus. Smitty and I returned to the Kaserne just before the mess hall closed for breakfast. After breakfast, we cleaned up and headed out to the service club. We had enough time to have a cup of coffee before the bus was to leave. Looking around the room, it seemed as if the bus would be complete. I'm glad we made our reservations ahead of time.

One of the ladies in charge of the trip announced that everyone on this tour should board the bus. We got on the bus and sat toward the end of the bus. The bus ride was to be about two hours long, with only one stop for bathroom use and picking up some refreshments. The distance from Lenggries to the Castle was about 160 K's, one hundred miles away.

As we spotted the castle, there was some excitement on the bus, people pointing toward the Alps and seeing the castle from this distance. The bus stopped at the little village named Hohenschwangau at the base of the mountain town. We received a little speech and directions from the tour director.

To get to the Castle, we had to walk up the winding road to the top of the high hill where the Castle sat. Wouldn't you know there were more places where we could sit and drink beer? Smitty and I sat for a few minutes to drink a fast beer; we didn't want the rest of the tour to leave us behind. When the beer arrived at our table, we downed it, left the money on the table, and walked quickly to catch up with the rest of the tour.

There were long lines to enter the Castle; maybe there were about 25 people at a time, a group to advance into the castle. It was a great and beautiful building, and the tour guides were very informative about the history of the Castle. There was lots of great information to hear about this Castle. There was a small souvenir shop in the Castle and souvenir shops on the way back down the mountain. The tour was about an hour long. We headed back off the mountain to the bus that would take us back to Lenggries and then to the barracks.

The first call was on Monday morning and another day at school. The classes were intense; all I had to remember was to place my notes in the textbook because our exams were open books. The instructor would let us have an open book test because when we were to work on some radio equipment, we'd have our books with us if needed.

In the following days, I spent much of my time doing classroom work and some studying after hours. Taking a break from studying, I went to the service club again. Sure enough, I saw June there. She spotted me and didn't waste time coming over to see how I was. We sat and talked, and she seemed interested in me for some unknown season. Did she like me? I am twenty years old and had one thing in mind, and I'm sure she had the same on her mind. I asked June if she wanted a soft drink; when she said sure, I went to pick up a couple of sodas. While sipping on the sodas we discussed the last time we were together, she reminded me of the good time she had a few days before. She was correct; I also had a good time with her. I wasn't looking for a steady girl because I would be here briefly. After school, I would go back to Friedberg in the communication squad.

June asked if I would walk with her while it was still daylight outside. I went out with her, and we headed toward the main gate. After we got away from the Kaserne, June grabbed my hand and locked our fingers together. We might have walked about a mile when we came upon a park bench away from the street. Once we sat, we embraced in a hot, wet kiss that lasted about five minutes. We pulled apart and talked about our short time together, and I was hopeful she was being honest with me. June told me she was interested in having a good time as I was and nothing serious. That was fine with me, and that was our decision. We'd be friends during the remainder of my stay in radio school. June and I decided to get together on Saturday to drive in her father's car to Bad Tolz for dinner. Maybe even take a trip up Brauneck Mountain by cable car. It was a date; we headed back to Kaserne. While walking back, we stopped a few times to kiss and fondle each other.

When we arrived at the Kaserne, I returned to the barracks, and June headed to the service club. When I arrived at the company, I went to the day room, and maybe I'd find someone to play a few pool games before calling it a night. I took a cue, racked the balls, and asked if anybody would like to play a game. One of the guys at the other end of the room was interested and came over to play. While playing, I asked him if he knew June, who hung out at the service club. He started laughing to no end and told me she was nothing but trouble.

The next few weeks passed before I realized classes were over, and it was time to head back to Friedberg. I was just about at the bottom of the course and was never very interested in any school. I packed my bags the next day and left for Ray Barracks in Friedberg.

Chapter Thirty-One
Transfer to Brigade

Arriving back at the company barracks in Friedberg, I went to my room in the communications platoon to unpack my bags. Not long after that, the First Sergeant called me to the orderly room. He was upset because I had a low grade at the radio school, though I had passed. After a long talk, I was dismissed and went to the communications room in the basement where the crew was. Despite everything, I was able to keep up with my current job. After the last daily formation, we headed to the motor pool for the daily radio check. After dinner, I went to see my old squad members. We talked about what we could do that evening. If it weren't going to the club, we'd go to the Bahnhof Bar in town. We decided to go into town for a few drinks and play a few foosball with the Germans.

The following day, during work formation, I was ordered to KP for the next day, and on Saturday, I would be on motor pool guard duty. I could tell I was being targeted because I had been the last in my radio school class; someone had to be the last in the class, even though I was a driver and was supposed to be exempt from KP and guard duty. The First Sergeant was still angry because I had dropped out of NCO Academy.

A few weeks passed, and I was on extra duty about 20% of the time. The motor pool sergeant noticed I wasn't showing up to the motor pool every evening like I had been. He called me aside and told me he could see what was happening and that he had heard about an opening for a jeep driver for the Brigade Commander Colonel Drake. All I had to do was apply. The next day, I took a few minutes and went over to Brigade Headquarters, just a few buildings away. I went straight to the Colonel's office to apply for the job. I knocked on the door, but there was no answer, so I went to the Sergeant Major's office and asked about the jeep driver position. The first question asked was, "Where are you from, Soldier?" When I told him I was from Maine, he said, "You have the job." He then told me that Maine people knew how to drive in all weather conditions. He asked me to return when the Colonel was in his office for an interview.

I went to the motor pool to see the sergeant, who had told me about the jeep driver job, and to let him know I had an interview. As I approached the office, the Sergeant saw me entering the building. He came over and told me he had received a call from the Sergeant Major about me applying for the Colonel's driver job and wanted me to get a driver's license for every vehicle in the motor pool. The Sergeant asked for my license, took it from me, and stamped and approved a permit for all vehicles in the motor pool.

I was getting a new job, and it called for a celebration. That evening, I signed up for a pass to visit Gil at the division headquarters. We were going to the Topper Club for a couple of drinks. Going to the Topper Club was, in a way, relaxing—sitting there and drinking our worries away. I think this was the first time I worried about my job in the Army. I told Gil about having the lowest grade in my class. I felt like a failure, but Gil was there to cheer me up, and he did. It was getting late, and I wanted to return to the Barracks before midnight. Gil and I parted. He took the bus back to Drake Kaserne, and I took the trolley car to the Bahnhof and the train back to Friedberg. I walked from the Bahnhof to the barracks, which took about a twenty-minute walk.

The next day, I went to Brigade for the job interview with Colonel Drake for the jeep driver's job. I first saw Sergeant Major Blessing and asked him for hints on approaching the Colonel. He had me all prepped up for the interview within a few minutes. I knocked on his office door when I heard him say, who is it? I entered and reported to him. I had newly starched clothes and just had my boots spit-shined. The Colonel motioned to the chair and told me to have a seat, which I did. We talked for about half an hour, and I must have made a good impression as he told me the job was mine. The Colonel had me stop by Sergeant Major Blessing to get my orders to transfer to my new job as the Colonel's jeep driver. Again, I would be exempt from any extra duties.

When I arrived at the barracks, the first sergeant inquired about me. I believe the brigade must have informed him that I had requested that I be transferred to the brigade headquarters. The first Sergeant was upset at me; I had broken the chain of command. The First Sergeant told me to pack my stuff and return the equipment that was issued to me by this company. I went to see the guys and said that I had requested a transfer to Brigade and got it, and I was moving this very day. I called

Sergeant Major Blessing to see if he could arrange transportation for me and my personal belongings, which he did.

The room I was attached to had about a dozen beds in it. The room was large enough that all beds were on the floor with no bunks on each other, like from 1/36. Brigade headquarters would be my home for the next three or four months.

The mess hall was only the next building from the one I was staying in. One Sunday afternoon, I went over for lunch, and to my surprise, I had to sign up for my meal. In the two years I've been in the Army, signing for my meals was the first time I had to sign for a meal. I was curious about why; I found out that some of the cooks and kitchen staff were taking food from the mess hall straight to the trunk of their cars and taking it to their homes or towns on the black market. Many people were involved in the black market in Germany during the sixties. Even I sold my cigarettes to the guy at the record store in town, Friedberg.

Racial disturbances were happening in the military community in the sixties. It wasn't a good time for the troops, and it came to a point nobody could trust one another. We had to work together. It wasn't too bad while on duty, but if we were to go into town or the city (Frankfurt), we were ordered to be on our best behavior. Once, a friend and I were in Friedberg and entered the Gasthaus. There were no white people in the place except for the employees. The bartender asked us to leave the club. We gave him no problem as we could see why, and then we left the Gasthaus.

Another time, one of my friends went home on leave to New Jersey; when he returned, he told me he had been shot in the arm by a national guardsman during a riot. Holy shit, that must have been scary.

Many African American soldiers moved over to one building one weekend and moved all others out. I didn't want to get involved in any disagreements with anybody. That weekend, I just left the Barracks and went to stay with Gil in Frankfurt.

Chapter Thirty-Two
Emergency leave

For the first time, I saw things from a different perspective of what I had already learned from being in a line of infantry. I moved from an infantry line company and skipped the battalion, going straight to the brigade headquarters. Life was a little easier in my new job. As the driver to the Brigade Commander, I always had to be ready for the Colonel. I also had plenty of time for other duties, as he only needed me mostly when we went to the field. Marshall was his sedan driver, and he was required most of the time.

One of my first assignments at Brigade Headquarters was to set up for testing some of the infantry companies in the field. We had a couple of days before we would depart for the training. That evening, a few of us decided to go to the club after work duty; we'd had dinner there. Heineken beer was my favorite; I would drink three or four of those a night. I tried to limit myself to no more than two beers a night, another great addition to my Army years.

After eating at the club, I noticed Layton and Victor at the other end of the club. I went over to see them and sat with them for a few minutes, well, at least enough time to have another beer. Now that I was no longer with the line infantry, Layton and Victor wanted to discuss the night I lost my virginity. We never talked about that night in detail, and they just wanted to know how my night with the girl from the snack bar was. It was when Layton informed me that he had paid the girl to see that I had a good time. I told Layton that I did get his money's worth. I told Layton and Victor we didn't get too much sleep that night, and I never knew sex could be so fantastic after hearing my mother for years telling me that sex was evil. Layton and Victor wanted me to go into details, which I would not do. I did tell them we had sex six times during the night we were together. Layton was more like a big brother to me, a mentor. He taught me much about military life; he had served two tours in Vietnam. Layton and Victor told me not to be a stranger as I was leaving. Finishing my beer, I returned to the table with the guys from my new company.

After drinking another beer, I left the club and went to the barracks. As I entered the room, I noticed a few of the guys playing poker. The first words out of my mouth were asking if I could sit in; I love a good game of poker. We did not play for cash, but we did play for cigarettes. I wasn't much of a smoker and didn't start until I entered the Army. Six of us played cards, and it seemed as if I couldn't lose a game. The stars must have been with me that night. One of the players had a bottle of whiskey, and we were all drinking out of the same bottle. By the time we stopped playing, I must have won about ten cartons of cigarettes, all loose in a large paper bag. I was drunk that night and did a stupid thing; I dumped the whole bag of cigarettes from the third-floor window.

Getting up the following day with a hangover and making a police call after formation was a bitch. I made many enemies that morning; we had to pick up all those cigarettes. I learned my lesson: don't throw anything out of the window. After policing the area, we headed to the mess hall and had to prepare for the field infantry testing. I spent time in the motor pool making sure my Jeep was up to par, and I loved keeping a neat and clean vehicle. When the evening came, I decided to go to the movies to watch "The Happenings." I watched the film with a friend from the 1/36th. While watching the show, I received a notification from the PA system. The information was for me to call the Red Cross as soon as possible. I left the movie theater and went to the barracks' orderly room to reach the Red Cross. The information I received from them was that I had an aunt who had passed away that afternoon.

The Red Cross did all they could to get in touch with Gil and me, who was in Frankfurt, to get a flight back home. I called Gil, and we put our plans together. The Red Cross had tickets for us on the same flight home to Maine. We were to leave in the A.M. from Frankfurt airport. My section leader allowed me to go that night, and I would stay in Frankfurt with Gil and leave together in the morning.

Going Stateside meant I could not participate in the testing, and it didn't bother me in the least. I rushed back to the club, hoping to catch Layton and Victor and tell them I would go Stateside for a month. I did not want them to worry about why they would not see me around for a while. I returned to the barracks, started to pack, and left to head back to Frankfurt. Marshall was allowed to drive me to Frankfurt in the Colonel's sedan.

I arrived at Kaserne in Faranfurt. I went to Gil's room, and he found an empty bed for me for the night. We planned to leave the Kaserne right after breakfast to be at the airport by 1000 hours, as our flight departed at 1300 hours. After we visited for a while, we went to bed; it wasn't easy to fall asleep with all of this on my mind.

Due to our situation, Gil and I didn't have to attend reveille in the morning. Gil and I were up early with the rest of the men. He and I beat the rush to the mess hall for breakfast. After breakfast, we went to the barracks, picked up our bags, and then Gil signed out in the orderly room. We went to the front gate to catch a cab to take us to the airport, about a forty-minute drive. We had to watch the cab drivers; sometimes, they would try to bring you the long way around to add to the fare.

We got to the airport quickly; we checked in our bags and walked to a nearby restaurant to have a beer before boarding the flight to New York. Gil and I wore our class A uniform for this trip. I learned that traveling in uniform, we received a little honor from the older people, but from the younger folks, we would be treated like crap, especially by the college students.

The flight home was on time, and the flight went without interruption. We landed in New York as scheduled. Gil and I exited the plane and waited a few hours for our connecting flight to Maine. We went to a bar with bags in our hands to have a beer. I ordered a beer, and when Gil ordered one, they asked him for his ID. Now, here we were, both in Army uniforms, and the drinking age at the time was eighteen. Gil refused to reveal his identity, and the service to Gil was denied. I canceled my beer and left without any further beer.

We walked over to our departing gate and noticed a small food court where we sat and had a light lunch. Just as we finished our lunch, we heard on the public address system that our flight was boarding. We went over, and we boarded without any hesitation. We arrived in Portland, Maine, on time; the trip took about an hour and a half from New York. It wasn't long before we landed, and our parents were waiting for us at the gate.

Mom, Dad, and Rose, our sister, were happy to see us. Gil and I retrieved our luggage and headed to the car. It was about an hour's drive home from the airport. Mom explained to Gil and me how our aunt had died. The burial was going to be in the morning. It's a shame to say, but it seems like the families only get together for funerals. Once at home, Gil and I took turns using the telephone to contact some of our friends. To our surprise, many were in the military and were not home.

Visiting hours at the funeral home were two hours in the afternoon and two hours in the evening. Mom started preparing lunch for us before we headed out to visit the funeral home. We arrived at the funeral home about one thousand feet from where we lived. Dad drove the car to the funeral home, even at that short distance.

Arriving at the funeral home, we waited in line to sign the guest book, and then we moved along to view my aunt Joan; she was very young, only forty-eight years of age. Aunt Joan and her husband, Uncle Bill, had six children. Uncle Bill was Mom's brother-in-law, and there were twelve siblings in Mom's family. I met cousins I had never met; still in uniform, Gil and I attracted much attention. We followed the Catholic rituals, and I was into Catholic beliefs.

After leaving the funeral home, our family went home; once at home, I got out of my Army uniform and changed into my street clothes. While being home for four weeks, I wanted to get a chance to see some of my school buddies who hadn't joined the military. Most of my high school friends had joined the Army. I hung around with one of my cousins, Margaret; she was a year younger than me. I could depend on her to find one of her friends to date me while I was home on leave.

It was January 1968, and there was snow on the ground. Gil and I would take turns using Dad's car, and Dad was good to us about letting us use his car as long as we brought it back full of gas. My older brother was already out of the Army and hadn't arrived home in Waterville. Jeff and his wife Kelly lived in Hartford, Connecticut, and would be in Waterville anytime. Gil and I had eighteen months to serve before being discharged from the Army. Later that evening, we returned to the funeral home with the rest of the family. Many family members visited Aunt Joan, who had twelve siblings and about forty nieces and nephews. Jeff and Kelly were home with their baby girl when we got home.

The following day, we were to attend the funeral at a Catholic Church in Waterville, Maine. That morning at home, we all got up early. With seven of us at home, it took time to get ready as there was only one bathroom, a bathtub, and no shower. We had enough time to clean up and have a good breakfast before leaving the house. We all left the house and headed to the funeral home. After the casket was closed at the funeral home, we could enter the cars and follow the lead vehicle. The funeral was held at St. Francis Church, packed with families and friends. It was a sorrowful day in our family's lives. After the funeral, we all gathered at a local church hall for a light lunch in memory of my aunt.

On Friday night, I went to a dance in Brewer at one of the Auditoriums. I went with one of my friends with whom I went to high school; His name was David. The trip to Brewer was a little over an hour's drive. Going to the dance was fun, but not as much fun as when I was still in high school. I was twenty years old, and everyone at the dance seemed younger than I was. A twenty-year-old doesn't ask a seventeen-year-old to dance. Three years was a significant difference at that age, and we left the dance early.

With about two weeks left on our leave, I thought I would check on Pam from Fairfield to see if she was still available for a date. I called Pam, and she was home and surprised to hear I was home. I asked if she wanted to go out with me as I had two weeks before Gil and I headed back to Germany. She was more than happy to hear from me and accepted my request for an evening date.

I picked Pam up at her home, then drove to the movie theater and watched a movie. I don't remember what movie we watched. Pam and I got very close in the theater's back row. Before the show was over, we left and drove toward Quarry Road behind Thayer Hospital to the Devil's Chair, a rock formation on a ledge shaped like a chair. I did get to fondle her breasts when she invited me by unbuttoning her blouse. Her breasts were nice and firm as I remembered them, and I let her go her way with me. After a little while, the car windows were all fogged. We climbed over to the rear seat to better enjoy our evening. Her top was wholly unfastened, exposing her skimpy bra. Her bra was around her neck. She laid down, and I unbuttoned my shirt and laid on her bare chest, and her bare breasts felt great. We dry-humped until she got off me when we spotted some lights at a distance. We straightened ourselves, and I took her to her home, then went home for the night.

Gil and I were taken to the Airport for our journey to Frankfurt as our leave ended. We left Portland, Maine, and our first stop was Logan International Airport in Boston, MA. Not long after arriving at the airport, we heard the PA system announcing the boarding of our flight. We said our goodbyes, shared hugs and kisses, then walked to the boarding gate. Gil and I sat close to the plane's rear and the toilets.

The airplane landed in Boston, and we only had a few minutes to catch our connecting flight. We got off the plane and headed to the new departing gate. Gil and I just carried our carry-on bags, and the airline personnel took care of our larger bags about forty-five minutes earlier before our departure across the great big pond. When we arrived at the departing gate, we sat down in the waiting area as there were a few more minutes before boarding.

Here is the announcement we've been expecting. I loved living in Germany, a long distance from Maine, but it was my new home after over two years. We boarded the plane, and Gil and I moved again to the aircraft's rear. We talked about how I could transfer to Frankfurt, 3rd Armored Division; we decided to work on that when we returned home (Friedberg).

Chapter Thirty-Three

Transfer to Division Headquarters

Arriving back to the Brigade after the long trip from home in the States and settling back into my room, I went to see Sergeant Major Blessing. I asked him again for a transfer request (1049) to Division Headquarters. The Sergeant Major told me he would remove the submission if I applied again. I left his office and went on with my daily duties.

In the next few days, I thought of ways to get a transfer to Division Headquarters. Payday was just a few days away, and it would be an excellent time for me to head out to Frankfurt after work and see if Gil's boss could help me with a transfer. I knew we were not supposed to break the chain of command, but I broke it for the second time and had to go above the broken link.

Every payday, I would go down to Bad Nauheim, next town from Friedberg. I'd go to the American Express office to pay for the loan I had taken out for a plane ticket I purchased for a trip home. Using my monthly rations, I'd also stop at the PX in Bad Nauheim to buy four cartons of cigarettes. On returning to the barracks, I'd stop at Friedberg's local record store to purchase 45 RPM records. While looking around at the different records, the shop manager approached me again and asked if he could see me in his back office. I went along with him to see what he wanted. It wasn't my first time in this shop, so he did recognize me from past visits.

The shop owner had asked me if I'd be interested in selling my cigarettes to him again. He told me he'd offer fifty Marks a carton like last time. That sounded very profitable, but I knew this would be a black market if I sold him cigarettes. I had paid a dollar per carton at the PX. He wanted to give me two hundred Marks for the four cartons. I left his office empty-handed and with a pocket full of cash. Black marketing was the only time I had done anything like this, with two hundred Marks, about fifty US dollars. I could always buy a few packs of cigarettes from some of the guys on post.

The record shop wasn't too far away from the Paprika Restaurant, right next to the town's Castle. It being noontime, I went to the Paprika for some lunch. The food there was excellent, and the menu had many options. While I was having lunch, Roberts, a member of my infantry unit, walked in and asked to sit with me. I motioned for him to take a seat.

After Roberts and I had lunch, we decided to walk about three miles to the base. We walked for maybe an hour, so off we went. Roberts told me he was looking for a way to get out of the infantry unit like me. Roberts was being harassed at the company by some members of his platoon. He told me he wanted to leave that unit so badly that he even requested 1049 to Vietnam. I felt terrible for Roberts, but he wasn't the only one headed to war. When we arrived back at base, it was almost time for the last formation before heading to the motor pool for a communications check.

That afternoon after work, I changed into civvies and headed out to Frankfurt. I didn't even take the time to hit the mess hall. I wanted to see Gil's boss to see if he could help me, as he had asked me a few times when I would be moving to Frankfurt. When I got to Division Headquarters, I hurried to find Gil. His company clerk in the orderly room told me he was still at his office. When I got to the office, I asked Gil if his boss was still there. He was, so I knocked on his door. When I entered, I reported in, and he told me to relax, as he knew who I was. We talked for a while about why I wanted to see that today. After telling the colonel, Sergeant Major Blessing ripped my transfer request. He was pissed off. The Colonel informed me that when requesting a transfer request, the request must be completed in the system, even if rejected.

The Colonel told me not to worry; he would approve a transfer for me, and I would be transferred to headquarters. I thanked him, told him he had made my day, saluted him, and left. I returned to see Gil and told him I would be in Frankfurt soon. Gil finished his work, and we headed to the mess hall for dinner. After that, we went to the EM club for entertainment, as there was live entertainment that night.

A young singer from the UK was singing with an accompanying local band. She was an excellent singer. She sang "RESPECT" by Aretha Fraklin, and they rocked the club that night. After a couple of beers, I left to head back to Friedberg. I was anxious about the transfer to division HQ. When I returned to base, I went to my room for the night—I needed a good night's rest.

The following day, during reveille, my platoon leader informed me that Sergeant Major Blessing wanted to see me ASAP. I knocked on his door, entered upon his command, and could see he was upset with me for my actions.

He wanted to know why I broke the chain of command regarding my transfer to Headquarters. I told him that what he had done by ripping up my transfer was wrong, and I mentioned it to my brother's boss, and he told me you were in the wrong. He had me come to his desk and handed me some papers to sign. I read the documents, and they were for the transfer. Sergeant Major Blessing told me to pack my bags, that he would have someone take me to the Division Headquarters in Frankfurt ASAP, and that I was never to return to the Third Brigade headquarters. He was upset that I had broken the chain of command. I never asked Gil's boss for the transfer—he took it upon himself because my brother had mentioned to his boss that he had orders to be in Friedberg when he arrived in Germany.

Gil's boss told him his MOS was needed more at the Division Headquarters level than in an infantry unit. He then said he would do anything to have me there. It didn't take long; Gil and I shared the same room when I arrived. All of this time, the Colonel was waiting for my transfer papers to show up, but they never did.

My new job at Division Headquarters was for G3 Supply, along with a few other duties. One of the tasks was going to the V Corps building in the city to have classified materials burned in their incinerator—I did this once a week. On the days I would have to go to V Corps to burn classified materials, I'd go to the motor pool, sign out a jeep, and recruit someone to accompany me. We'd pick up classified trash that had to be destroyed by fire. We headed down to V Corps. Once we arrived at V Corps, we went to the incinerator to deposit the trash. We watched through a small window to ensure only ashes were left. Of course, there was a paper trail. Whenever classified material was moved and exchanged, I needed signatures to show the material was disposed of correctly.

My primary assignment was driving an expandable van to house the central operations office when we went into the field. We'd park four to six vans parked next to each other in the field. Then, we'd set up a platform to connect all the vans, creating a layout that looked like a group of offices with a hallway.

Being stationed here in Frankfurt has to be the best duty I have had so far. Coming from central Maine, I wasn't used to having everything in the same city. You could do anything you imagined in Frankfort. A person didn't need a car, with buses, trolleys, trains, and available to get around.

Gil and I had different friends but still did many activities together. I felt good about having Gil in Germany with me. Gil's work involved getting to know all the top brass in Division Headquarters; he and I got away with many things during our year stationed there.

Chapter Thirty-Four
Field Training

With the next field maneuver, which would take place soon for Gil and me, this would be the first time we would be out on training together. Gil and I would have to drive our trucks and trailers with the advance party to set up our equipment and office spaces for the training period. I hadn't realized Gil had a truck driver's license as he, being a clerk, was surprised he could also drive a truck.

A few days before going on this field problem, Gil told me he had a WAC (Woman's Army Corp) friend at Gibbs Kaserne station next to the General Hospital in Frankfurt, near our post. Gil first met her at advanced training in Indianapolis. Gil called her to see if she wanted to go out and if she could find a date for me. Things worked out, and we doubled-dated that night.

Later that afternoon, Gil and I prepared to take these girls out and hopefully have a great time. We stopped by the PX on the way out of the main gate to pick up some condoms, just in case. Outside the main entrance on Hamburgerlandstrass was a bus stop, bus number 63, which would take us straight to Gibbs Kaserne. We didn't have to wait too long for the bus. Once we reached their barracks, we went to the company orderly room, where we waited for them to come down to be with us. Gil told the girls what time we'd pick them up after work. We weren't there for just a few minutes before they showed up. The girls looked outstanding as they walked into the room. Gil's friend, nicknamed Mouse, must have been because she was a tiny woman. The other girl, who was about to be my blind date, was called Magie. I'm glad I wasn't blind, as she was gorgeous.

We left their company area and walked to the trolley stop to catch it and head toward the city center. After several stops, we exited the trolley and walked to the subway station. We rode the subway to the front of the train station. It was just a few minutes before we arrived downtown in the Kaiser Strasse area. We went into one of our favorite night spots; it was a great bar and a restaurant hall. The place was huge; it even had a balcony, and lamps and phones were on each table, and each lap had a number on it. The reason behind that was if you wanted to ask someone for a dance, all you had to do was give the table a call, and if you were lucky, you'd get a dance without having to ask anyone face to face.

We found a table for the four of us, and it wasn't long before we had some beers on the table that we had ordered. After the beers were on the table, the waitress took our order for our dinner. While waiting for our dinner, my date and I got to know each other better. Magie was from Texas, had dark brown hair, and looked lovely and shapely. While waiting for our meal, Maggie and I went to the dance floor to get a dance in before our dinner arrived. When we arrived at the dance floor, the band played a slow song for a slow dance. We were side by side as we started dancing, talking, and slowly moving. We spoke and moved slowly; within a minute, Magie took both of my hands and pulled me close to her until our bodies touched. I could feel her firm body against mine, and at this time, our faces were almost touching, so I moved in a little closer and planted a small kiss on her lips. When I planted a small peck on her lips, she pulled me even closer. She shoved her tongue into my mouth, and we swapped some spit. The song ended, and we separated and walked to our table while still holding hands.

Gil and Mouse had already started to enjoy their dinner. Magie and I sat, and we enjoyed our meal while we kept on talking. Both of us looked excited. I wasn't paying much attention to Gil and his date, Mouse. After we had finished our meals, Magie and I returned to the dance floor. I believe both Magie and I enjoyed each other's company. We danced slowly with every song played, we both enjoyed it very much. We both had roaming hands, and she could tell I enjoyed her company as I enjoyed her company. Magie, being so close to me, could feel my manhood pressing against her thigh. I think we broke a record for having the most extended kiss. There wasn't much talking.

I felt someone's hand on my back when I turned around to check who was trying to get my attention. It was Gil and Mouse on the dance floor next to us. We swapped dance partners for a couple of dances to get to know each other's dates.

As time passed, we noticed it was getting late; Gil and I had to get up early the following day to prepare to leave Frankfurt for the field problem in a few days. We left the hall and halted down a cab to get a ride to Gibbs, where the girls lived. Gil, Mouse, and I sat in the back, and Magie sat in the front. Magie positioned herself so I could advance and kiss her from the back seat. My hands were all over her with her blouse unbuttoned halfway down. I was able to massage her perfectly rounded breasts. Gil and Mouse were also exceptionally good at it.

When we arrived at Gibbs, we all got out of the cab, and I paid the driver, and off they went. Gil and I were to walk back the rest of the way to our base, about 2 miles away. We were saying goodnight to the girls and asking if we could hook up with them when we returned from our field problem. To our surprise, the girls said they only went out with us that night because Mouse knew Gil. When we started to walk away, Magie grabbed Mouse's hand and pulled Mouse to her and locked lips, and Mouse said to us that they were gay. We never saw them again.

We turned away from the girls and headed back to our base. We took a shortcut through a Cemetery to save some time. Walking through the cemetery was very dark as there were no lights. Gil was following me, and suddenly, I heard a cry from Gil. Help me was what I heard, so I turned around but could not see Gil as he had fallen into a freshly dug grave. After helping Gil out of the grave, we laugh about him falling into a hole.

The following day, Gil had to work at his office before going to the motor pool to check on the truck; he would be driving out on the advance attachment team. Right after the work call, I headed out to the motor pool to check out my truck to ensure all our communication equipment was operational for our trip out into the field. I opened the van at the motor pool by extending out the sides. I had to use a crank to expand the Vans' sides. After the expansion of the truck, it measured 12 feet by 24 feet wide, with dividers to create rooms. Gil and I stayed in the barracks going over our list. We took some time to go to the PX to stock up on snacks and soft drinks. Having collected our belongings for this movement, we were ready to go at the end of the evening.

The first call sounded, and we went out for the morning formation; we got our regular morning instructions. This morning would be our last meal in the mess hall for a few days. After breakfast, Gil, the rest of the company personnel, and I headed out to the motor pool to prepare to make sure our convoy was ready for the field. As always, this morning was one of those hurry-up and wait times.

Finally, after we waited to hit the road for a couple of hours, we started to move out. We must have driven for about three hours before we reached our destination. We set up on the outskirts of a small village in the forest, away from the road. Gil and I had to set up tents for the Officers' sleeping quarters. Gil wasn't familiar with putting up a tent as he was a clerk, but the men he worked with did well. I set up my boss's tent and then had to set up the truck in the communication post.

The cafeteria was all setup, and we finished setting up our tents and truck for operations. Lunch was ready; we could smell the food as it was cooking. We all headed toward the mess hall for our dinner. After dinner, as part of the advanced party, we had a meeting to plan for the next day as the training was about to start. The officers had arrived, and they checked their tents to make sure it was to their satisfaction. The officers wanted Gil and me to place oil-heating stoves in their tents and get them lit to keep their tents warm and toasty.

I didn't have any problem setting up the oil stove. I lit up the burner, and it wasn't long before the tent was warm. I checked to see how Gil was doing with his tent, and he seemed to have done an excellent job. After the tents were up, with the stoves, the tents were getting nice and warm for the officers. Then we headed to the mess tent for dinner.

After dinner, Gil and I checked the tents to ensure everything was good. Gil came running over to me and told me he may have screwed up because the stove was running hot. It caught the tent on fire, and was able to put the fire out with a fire extinguisher within minutes. After confirming with his colonel that the fire had caused the fire, Gil was then ordered to set up another tent in the same area. It was good that the Colonel had not yet relocated any of his items in the tent.

It was dark out, and Gil had to put up a second tent without using any lights as we were in training mode. Gil had set up another tent successfully without using lights to see what he was doing. Gil did have a couple of troops help him. In the morning, Gil came over to see me and asked if I could help him straighten out the tent he had set up in the dark. Gil did not use any tent pegs to secure the tent, and most of the rope support was inserted into tree branches; the tent was a spider web. Within a few minutes, all was good. I found out how the tent was scorched. The oil burner stove was missing the oil filter, which controlled the oil flow. Gil had learned his lesson on how to set up a tent and oil burner.

The training was very tense for the next three days and nights. Most troops involved in these training exercises didn't get much sleep. There was much eating and sleeping on the go, no rest for the wicked.

After three training days, the company personnel returned to the base and kept our field base intact. I volunteered to stay behind by my section leader's orders, who gave me a choice of who to keep with me and five others to say back to. I kept a cook so we'd have someone to make meals for us. I kept a communication person to operate our radios and a mechanic so we could use our jeep in case of an emergency if we had problems with our jeep. The last two people I kept with us were Unit Police, who were attached to our company while in the field. I hoped I could have had a medic, but I couldn't.

The last of the troops had left for Division headquarters in Frankfurt. I was pulling my troops together and instructing all five of them on our jobs for the weekend. That's right, and it was guard duty in the field. One of the things I told the troops was I would let two people team at a time to drive around our perimeter and check out all of the tents and vehicles in the area. I set up two-person teams with 6-hour shifts around the clock.

It was a Friday night, and I assigned one unit of police and the mechanic on the first round in the jeep, and the rest would stay at the camp to secure the camp for the night. Radio communication was a must so that I could be aware of everything. I had my tent as a command center, constantly communicating openly with Headquarters in Frankfurt. It was about 2200 hours. The cook and I walked around the camp to ensure all was secured and safe from the elements.

The cook and I took about one and a half hours to complete our walk through the encampment. Not long after our walk around, the two others in the Jeep arrived and reported to me. All looked good throughout the camp; the two on duty with the jeep took a side trip into the village about 3 miles away and stopped to pick up a case of flip-tops. Before the two took off in the jeep, I did mention that it was possible to pick up some beer and gave them money to cover the cost.

We sat telling stories for the rest of the evening and drank some good old German beer. For the next few hours, we learned about each other and where we were all from and became closer friends. It wasn't long before we heard a motor vehicle in the camp area. I went outside the tent and saw a car driving through the site. I approached the driver as he had stopped his vehicle, and the driver was walking toward me. I told the German he was in an off-limit area as this was a US Military training area. He apologized, returned to his car, and left the area.

After the last beer, I ordered the crew to do another walk around the camp. We all participated in this round and completed the tour. It wouldn't take too long with only two people. When we finished our walk-through, I assigned each of us a two-hour time watch, including me. Off to bed I went; there was nothing like sleeping in tents in sleeping bags with our clothes entirely on.

Early the following day, the cook was the first to get out of bed so he could prepare our breakfast for the rest of the crew. Nothing out of the extraordinary while we were out here on guard duty. The day duty wasn't hectic as only six of us were at the camp, and I was in charge. We had a small fire to heat water from our steel pot helmets. Heated water to get washed up; it was mainly like a sponge bath. After we were cleaned up and dressed for the day, I assigned duties to two troops, and the two did night watch. I gave them until noon to sleep. After breakfast, the cook and I took off in the jeep to run around the compound. We had left our weapons at the campsite, locked up in the same tent I had made into our little field office, with one of the troops keeping guard on the guns and operating the radios.

After making the rounds of the campsite, we headed to the small village the others had visited last night. I had the cook stop at a small Gasthaus to see what kind of entertainment they might have at night. I would let three troops go to this village on Saturday night, and the rest of us would go to the same Gasthaus on Sunday night. After entering the Gasthaus, we met the bartender, who pointed to the beer tap as if asking if we wanted one. We did attract attention with our jeep parked outside and dressed in full-field equipment. The proprietor greeted us at the table and told us the beer was on him, as with other places we had visited. We were attracting customers to his business site. I did notice some of the guests entering the Gasthaus were looking at us, and we could tell they were talking about us.

After we had drunk our free beer, we ordered a light lunch to take out with us. I love eating German food cooked by German cooks. We noticed a couple of girls looking and smiling at us, and I smiled back at the girls, who might have been about 30 years old. They smiled back at me. I got up, walked over to their table, and asked if they spoke English. One of the girls spoke a little English, and I wondered if we could sit with them at their table for lunch. They giggled and motioned for us to sit at their table.

Before we left, we asked for their names, and they wrote their names, Petra and Jennifer, on a napkin. As we stood up to go, the girls reached out their hands to welcome a warm handshake, a warm handshake it was. As we were leaving, the proprietor waved his hand, and we waved back, then out the door, we went. We got back into the jeep and drove off to our command post.

We arrived back at the camp at about 1300 hours. The cook went to the mess tent to prepare a fast meal for the other guys. The cook made them some sandwiches and some hot coffee for everyone. The rest of the day was routine, ensuring everything was secure and onlookers did not enter our field base.

We spent some time taking turns doing watch duty, and the rest of us who didn't do watch duty were playing cards. After playing cards for a few hours, some guys asked if they could take a jeep to the village to visit the Gasthaus, which we had been to the night before. With two nights left here on guard duty.

After returning to the tent with the beer, I allowed the troops on watch duty to take the jeep to drive around the camp to ensure the camp was safe and secure. After our last meal of the day, I gathered everybody together and assigned the teams their duties for the evening. With three troops going to the village and the three remaining, two team members would do the rounds on foot, and I would stay with the radios as we had to staff them at all times. I always had a two-way radio to keep in touch with the base while away from the camp.

That evening, the communication person, the mechanic, and one of the Unit Police went to the Village and headed to the Gasthaus as planned. After the three left, I wandered around the campsite doing extra checks to ensure all was secured and safe. Around 2100 hours, I went to bed; I slept with my 45 under my pillow for protection. I heard what sounded like a motorcycle not far from my tent. I had a light on inside the tent. The motorcycle engine had stopped, and I heard footsteps outside the tent. I yelled out identity yourself, and a person spoke out. I got up and looked out of the tent, and it was a German looking for a particular person. I asked him why, and he told me he had found a wallet and wanted to return it. It had a person's name on it. He gave it to me, and I thanked him, and he left.

The next morning, I gathered the team to plan our day's work. I remembered this would be the day the rest of our group from headquarters would be back. We expected the company to arrive at about 1000 hours on Monday morning, and we had to have the mess tent ready to feed the group as planned. We were to make sure that all were in a specific situation before they arrived. I would stay with the cook and help him to prep for Monday. The advanced team would arrive at about 0600 hours to ensure all was ready for testing, starting Monday evening as night training.

The cook, myself, and one of the UPs would take the time to spend a couple of hours at the Gasthaus. As I told the two girls we had met, I would be back to spend time with them. Everything was going well at the campsite. After the cook finished his work, one Police personnel and I took off in the jeep. We drove around the little village to get a few beers for the rest of the team for the evening.

Back at the camp, I radioed headquarters to check on how all was going and made plans for their morning arrival. All the information was as planned before the company left on Friday. There is nothing wrong with making sure all is on schedule. When evening fell upon us, we prepared to head out to town. As this would be the last night, we could visit the Gasthaus in the village. When we arrived at the Gasthaus, the girls were waiting for us. The UP (unit police) personnel didn't want to enter the Gasthaus, so he stayed outside and returned to the camp. I had given him orders to pick us up in two hours in front of the Gasthaus.

We entered and went straight to where the two girls were sitting. We ordered beers and got acquainted with the girls; they spoke broken

English, and we got along just fine. After a couple of beers, I went to the jukebox and dropped in a Mark to Play a few songs. When I returned to the table, I asked one of the girls if she wanted to dance with me. Before I could finish my sentence, she was up, and we grabbed each other's hand and headed to the dance floor. Of course, I played slow songs; I'm sure that is what she expected. We danced and moved very slowly; our bodies were so close together that you couldn't pass a thread between them. I could feel the warmth from her body up against mine. I'm sure she also was aroused as much as I was.

She leaned into me as she planted a kiss on my lips, and I followed in return. I'm confident she could tell I was turned on. I knew I could not go any further than kissing and petting. We finished our two dances, and it was hard to walk back without anyone noticing me. We sat down again, but our chairs were a lot closer together. We petted each other and kissed till our lips were almost numb.

Before long, it was time to get back to the base. The cook and I left and met the Unit Police driver, who took us back to the base. When I returned, I walked through the camp area to ensure everything was on track.

Early in the morning, the troops started to arrive at the campsite. I was no longer in charge and passed my duties to the company commander. The training went well, and we were training at this site for the rest of the time. After a week's training, we all went back to Division Headquarters. The training was complete.

Chapter Thirty-Five

ETS Back to The States

It was about two weeks from my ETS (Estimated Time Served), which meant I would be relocated Stateside for the remainder of my stay in the Army. I received my orders this morning and was excited about returning home. I would take a month's furlough home before starting my new assignment at Fort Campbell, Kentucky.

My First Sergeant called me to the orderly room and told me I had to go out to the field as a driver for some second lieutenant. I told the First Sergeant that I had orders to ETS and had to clear the post and other military installations in Frankfurt. The First Sergeant told me I had to follow his orders and I should have two days to leave the post. I left his office and went to see my section officer; I knew he could help me get time off. My section leader, a Major, was also clearing post since he was rotating to the States as I was. The Major called my First Sergeant and gave me time off to clear the post as he did. First, the sergeant was upset with me, but I didn't care. I'd never see him again.

I was a short-timer and would act like one, carrying a clipboard and a short-timer stick. I had a few places in the city that I had to clear; maybe I could have cleared base in two days, but as a rule, everybody was getting two weeks to clear base, and I wanted my two weeks. For the next two weeks, I was exempt from any duties. I would miss Gil, but we both were getting discharged in about eight months. I had to take an inventory and get a list of places to clear for the rest of that day. I had been in Friedberg before serving at Division Headquarters in Frankfurt, so I had to clear a few places in the Friedberg area.

I went to Gil's office to see the crew and let them know that I had orders to get reassigned to the States. The team knew I was getting ready for rotation as I kept telling everybody my 36 months were almost over for this assignment. Now, I was getting excited about returning to the States for the duration of my enlistment, which was seven months. I didn't know what I would do on this next assignment at Fort Campbell.

After getting all the information I needed for my rotation, I would plan my last two weeks in Germany. The next day, I would visit Ray Barracks to clear a couple of offices and the post exchange. I also wanted to see some of my friends, who I left behind when I was re-assigned to Division Headquarters.

After breakfast, I left the orderly room. I headed to Friedberg and the Bad Nauheim area to clear their businesses like those I have done business with. A military bus traveled from base to base in Germany. I took the bus to Friedberg this time instead of taking the train. While there, I wanted to visit some friends if they hadn't rotated. Once I arrived at Ray Barracks at the bus depot, I went to the 1/36 Infantry and the communication room. Remember, I did drive the communication track for a few months. Fotter was still there, and Thomson had already rotated back to the States.

Fotter and I went to the post-snack bar to chat, and I was interested in who was still in the company. It's been almost a year and a half since I left the company, and few people I was with were still there. The majority of the soldiers were discharged from the military. Fotter himself was getting ready for his rotation back to civilian life. We ordered some lunch and soft drinks. I looked around to see if I could see the young lady who took my virginity away and see if she had returned to work here at this snack bar, but I didn't see her. She is one person I will never forget; I can close my eyes and still see her and me together in a new chapter in my life. Mary pissed me off because she gave me the clap, don't get me wrong, I had a great time with her that night; we made love all night.

After lunch, Fotter and I said goodbyes and parted, never to see each other again. I went to Brigade Headquarters to the communication section where I had worked, and everybody I had worked with had gone. I went to a few places on the post where I had done business to get cleared. After leaving, I visited the American Express office in Bad Nauheim. I went out the back gate and walked to the Bohnhoff, and many memories came back of the many times I walked this route drunk.

I stopped at the Bohnhoff Bar across the street from the station. I had a beer and didn't even see anyone I had remembered from when I frequented the establishment. I finished my beer and went across the street to catch the train to Bad Nauheim. The train ride might have been about five minutes from the Bad Nauheim station. I took a cab to the Post Exchange, where the American Express office was.

I had purchased airplane tickets here in the past, so I had to clear their office and have them sign my papers saying I owed them nothing. While there, I wanted to purchase something from Germany to take home to my mother as momentum. I saw a lovely German Coco Clock; I bought it. I know she'd be happy to receive the clock as she has asked me to get her one.

After leaving the PX, I took a cab to the Bohnhoff in Bad Nauheim and returned to Frankfurt. Having to pass through Friedberg to return to Frankfurt would be the last time I would travel this route. Just a thirty-minute ride left on this train, and I possibly never ride a train again here or in the States. Arriving back in Frankfort, I went outside the station, and there was a military bus stop where I would take back to Drake Kaserne. Once back on the post, I went to my room, and Gil was there as the workday was over. He and I went to the NCO club for dinner, Wienerschnitzel, with gravy and mashed potatoes.

After our dinner, we stayed at the club for a few beers. We headed back to the barracks after a couple of hours. Excited about my rotation back to the States, I took inventory of what I would take with me and what things I would have to leave behind when I returned to my room. During three years in Germany, I accumulated a few things. I gave some of my stuff to some of the guys, with Gil having the first choice.

It was hectic for the next few days. Many company troops had to go out into the field for special training. Gil, being the department clerk, didn't have to go out this time. His boss was a full-bird Colonel who was favorably in his court. After a long day, I went to bed, hoping I could get some sleep with this much excitement. The few beers I had drank earlier helped me fall asleep.

One afternoon, I went to the NCO club for lunch and met the club manager, Buck Sergeant, named Jones. We talked for a while, and when he found out I was a short-timer, he asked if I would be interested in making a few bucks for the little time I had left here in Frankfurt. He asked if I could do some painting at the club while most troops were out in the field. I told Sergeant Smith that I wasn't interested in the work. I asked Sergeant Smith how he could afford an expensive Motorcycle and a new car with an E-5 rank. Smith told me that every night, he would mark in the business books as he paid off a $75.00 jackpot to a lucky winner; there was no winner. He pocketed $70.00 every night. He also told me he got extra pay as a club manager for the additional duty. Jones asked me to keep this information quiet. He'd get article 15 and maybe face some stockade time. I told him not to worry as I was leaving Germany and would never see him again after this week.

Today, I cleared the post and all the places I had to go before departing West Germany. The troops had just arrived back from the field. A few wanted to get together on my last day before I left Germany. Gil, a few troops, and I went into the city to one of our favorite clubs about a block from the Bohnhoff. We had a great evening at the dance club. The guys wouldn't allow me to pay for any of the drinks, and they tried to get me drunk. Still, I wasn't going to let that happen as I was leaving in the morning for the Frankfurt International Airport. I didn't want to start my trip home with a hangover. All went well on my last day, and we returned to the barracks before 2300 hours. I finished packing, and for the 36 months I was stationed in Germany, I fit all my belongings in my duffel bag and one suitcase.

I woke up early on my last morning in Frankfurt, excited about going to the States with a 30-day furlough home. I did not make this morning's formation. After leaving the orderly room and signing out for the last time, I returned and said my goodbyes to Gil and a few guys. I headed out the front gate and hailed a cab.

Once in the cab, it would take about half an hour to get to Frankfurt Airport. The cab driver stopped me off in front of the TWA depot. I paid off the cab driver and entered the building; I went to the TWA counter and checked in my two bags. My flight was about three hours before departing, and I walked around looking for a nice German restaurant to eat my last German meal. I spotted a food court and noticed what looked like an enjoyable place to sit for a good lunch. I even had a place to watch all the passersby. After sitting down and getting my order, another Soldier entered the restaurant. He walked up to me and asked if he could join me. Both of us were in uniform as this was the mode of travel. We talked for a while, and he told me his name was Williams, and he was getting discharged from the Army.

I shook hands with Williams and wished him the best of luck with his future. I got up, paid for my lunch, and headed toward the departing gate. I waited in line for my ticket and finally entered the airplane.

The End

About The Author

Patrick Roy is a 77-year-old Cold War Veteran. He entered the United States Army in 1965, just a few days after he graduated from High School in a small central Maine town. Patrick had an older brother in the Army and a twin brother who joined the Army. Patrick served in many different capacities while he served. He was discharged from the Army in 1969 and married his childhood sweetheart a few months later. They raised two boys and have four granddaughters. Patrick has been pondering about writing a book for several years.

About Me

I, Patrick Roy, was born in 1947 in Maine to French parents. I did not learn to speak English until I was five years old. I grew up in a very low-income family with just bare necessities. I didn't have much while living at home, and I hoped joining the United States Army would improve my way of life, and it did. I've visited many European places in the three years I lived there in West Germany. I enjoyed West Germany so much that my wife and I have vacationed there eight times since marriage.

I married my childhood friend, and we have been married for 54 years. I have two incredible sons and four granddaughters. Life is what we make it.

www.ingramcontent.com/pod-product-compliance
Ingram Content Group UK Ltd.
Pitfield, Milton Keynes, MK11 3LW, UK
UKHW021904190726
13853UKWH00002B/507

9 798890 300300